Walter Lübeck

Reiki
For First Aid

Reiki treatment as accompanying therapy
for over 40 types of illness
With a supplement on natural healing

LOTUS LIGHT
SHANGRI-LA

Disclaimer

The information, instructions and recipes presented in this book have been carefully researched and passed on with the best intentions and to the best knowledge of the author. Nevertheless, the author and publishers accept no liability for damage of any nature resulting directly or indirectly from the application or utilization of information given in this book.

If you have any acute or chronic desease, please seek medical attention from a qualified doctor. Although the principles and practices presented here are beneficial in most cases, they should not be used as a means of clinical diagnosis or treating pathological conditions.

To avoid misunderstandings: The illustrations in this book show nude people for the purpose of a graphic description; however, this does not in any way indicate that Reiki treatment can or must be practiced without clothing.

1st English edition 1995
© by Lotus Light Publications
P.O. Box 325
Twin Lakes WI 53181, USA
The Shangri-La Series is published in cooperation
with Schneelöwe Verlagsberatung, Federal Republic of Germany
© 1990 reserved by Windpferd Verlagsgesellschaft mbH, Aitrang
All rights reserved
Translation by Samsara Amato-Duex
Editing by Christine M. Grimm
Cover design by Wolfgang Jünemann (Cover illustration by Berthold Rodd)
Artwork by Ute Rossow
ISBN 0-914955-26-8

Printed in the USA

Table of Contents

Introduction

In recent years, the USUI Reiki system has spread immensely throughout the world, particularly in America and Western Europe. The times at the turn of the century, when there was only a small committed group of Japanese involved, are long gone. In the beginning, this group was gathered around Dr. Mikao USUI, the first Grand Master and rediscoverer, and later around his successor Dr. Chujiro Hayashi and his Reiki clinics.

Since there is no record of all those who have participated in seminars, it is only possible to estimate how many people already practice Reiki. However, because of its high degree of success in healing and its easy, safe method of use even for people who are not medical professionals, Reiki has developed into a topic of increasing interest to the public.

Many books have already been published about Reiki, and courses on it are in demand. The USUI Reiki system is frequently passed on in two weekend seminars for the 1st (fundamentals) and 2nd degree (advanced), each consisting of 18 hours of instruction. Although these seminars are attended by many people who are not medical professionals, increasingly more doctors, healing practicioners, masseurs, physical therapists and psychologists participate. This means that broader segments of the population are becoming interested in Reiki for a variety of reasons.

Not necessarily every lay person possesses the specialized knowledge in the area of medicine or life energy to appropriately apply the home medical skills gained in a Reiki course as supportive therapy for serious health disorders or trivial illness. However, even professional healers such as doctors and healing practitioners grope somewhat in the dark when they use the universal life energy of Reiki at first, being limited by the inherent necessities of their daily work.

This is why I decided to write this book—my third—about this wonderful art of healing. My first book, "The Complete Reiki Handbook" (also available from Lotus Light/Shangri-La), describes Reiki therapy in theory and practice with comprehensive details. It can therefore be used at any time to add further depth to the methods mentioned in this current book. However, it is no longer a complete handbook because so many special usages for Reiki have developed. With *Reiki For First Aid*," this need can finally be fulfilled.

In order to primarily introduce new treatment forms here, I have consciously limited myself to a minimum of absolutely necessary information from my previous works on the same topic. This book is filled to the brim with new information! At the same time, to my knowledge this is the first time the direct connection between the application of Reiki and nutrition has been presented in detail. Nevertheless, it is not new. Dr. Chujiro Hayashi, the second Grand Master in the modern Reiki tradition, very intensively combined and researched the possibilities of achieving even more effectiveness from the application of Reiki in his Reiki clinics in Japan. Examples of these possibilities are suitable diets and water therapy, as well as psychological means.

Every individual, whether lay person or professional, can make good use of the information introduced here, discovering new dimensions of the Reiki system of healing for both himself or herself and others. I wish you much success and enjoyment with Reiki.

Walter Lübeck

Reiki
For First Aid

Chapter 1

How Does Reiki Heal?

In order to use Reiki creatively and employ it successfully under difficult circumstances, it is important to be thoroughly informed about the laws governing Reiki energy. These rules are valid for every level and for every application, from the laying on of hands in Reiki 1 to the Reiki 2 mental and absent treatments and to the initiation on the master/teacher level. They also apply to the combination with other methods, like aromatherapy and the work with healing stones.

The Seven Laws of Reiki Healing

1. Depending on a person's needs, the *inner child** draws Reiki into the disharmonies which exist on all levels of a human being's life. Reiki can never be forced onto or even pushed into a person in any way. Its effectiveness is independent for the most part of the faith or conscious will of the person being treated. Reiki is an offer that can be either accepted in different intensities and thereby perceived with a different healing effect by those who are treated—or it is not. Nevertheless, in

---

*The *inner child* is one of the three main functioning levels of every individual. In addition to other things, it is responsible for memories, feelings, vital life force, subtle perception, corporeality, love of life, ability to have relationships and subtle action potential. Its orientation is sensual and physical. The other two main functioning levels are: the *higher self,* responsible for holistic learning, personality development and the individual life plan of a person, as well as the *middle self* which is responsible for analytical-abstract thinking, habits, processing of sensory perception like sight, hearing, smelling, etc.; in addition, it controls all interactions on the material level. This model is based on the HUNA teachings, a very ancient Polynesian tradition of healing.

my practice I have never experienced an *inner child* that wouldn't accept any universal life energy at all. However, it can sometimes occur that Reiki energy cannot gain access to one area or the other of the body, soul or spirit or that it is only accepted after a longer period of treatment. Until this happens, these areas feel cold or even seem to not be capable of a reaction.

What exactly does the willingness of the *inner child* to use Reiki for itself depend upon? For one thing, it depends upon its perception of the direct use in its healing at the present moment. In other words, this means how far its desires for a symptom-free condition are being satisfactorily fulfilled under the current circumstances. Every illness has a deeper meaning for the person affected; it offers him or her a chance to become more conscious and allows the personality to continue in its growth. Or it creates a condition of balance (no matter how shaky) in order to remain capable of functioning. If the *inner child* has no possibilities at present to satisfy one or more of the uses mentioned, it will not exactly commit itself to making a contribution towards healing.

Further important aspects are trust in the person giving treatment, which means the freedom from fear and the feeling of safety, as well as the sense of being accepted within the therapeutic relationship. This point is obviously also true for self-treatment! If the *inner child* repeatedly experiences a rebuff from the *middle self* as soon as it lets its desire for sensuality, playfulness, joy of living, enjoyment and related feelings be known in a more intense manner, it won't readily reveal the sore points of its greatest sensibility, insecurity and vulnerability. A new trusting relationship must first be created before Reiki will be allowed adequate access in this case as well. The environmental circumstances should then also be taken into consideration. The more the client is bombarded with irritations, the more uncomfortable he or she feels in the treatment room, the less the *inner child* will open itself for Reiki. Based on these three conditions, it is possible to establish the following rules for the practical application of Reiki:

– The less deeply anchored in the psyche of the affected person it is, the more quickly and surely illness can be healed with Reiki.

– In order to successfully treat deep-seated illness, the body consciousness must be as convinced as possible of the economy of the healing; it must believe that this healing is connected with an improvement or at least a maintenance of its overall situation with respect to the fulfillment of its needs.

2. Reiki does not directly intervene in the body, but rather solely stimulates it to perceive its natural functions as extensively as possible. Reiki therefore does not represent an energy in the usual sense of the word because it cannot be classified as a particular quality like yin or yang, nor does it belong to a particular chakra. It is non-polar and for this reason it tends to represent an information which ultimately is best described as an "encouragement of liveliness." For the successful application of Reiki, it is then superfluous to pay attention to the polar assignment of the Reiki-user's hands to particular body zones of the person being treated. Reiki is not related to polarity in any way.

3. Reiki solely stimulates the body's own life-support and development potentialities; it does *not* directly affect the metabolism or the psyche. For this reason, particularly in cases of chronic, extensive illness, as well as those anchored in the mental structure, one must *additionally* provide an input which supports healing and growth: this means the appropriate nourishment, sufficient absorption of the best possible material quality and energetic quality of water, the appropriate stimulation for the promotion of learning and consciousness in accordance with the individual condition, as well as the neces-

sary strokes for body and soul. Similarly, it is an necessary to have an *output* that supports healing and growth. This includes bodily purification and detoxification in the broadest sense, in as far as the afflicted person can tolerate it. Furthermore, an appropriate vent for letting go of pent-up feelings is also important.

In order to guarantee the success of holistic healing, it is necessary to live out your own creativity, one of the most important phenomenon accompanying any holistic healing, and also engage in enough physical exercise to stimulate the metabolism. Accordingly, it means the unconditional acceptance of our own physical nature and the harmonious connection between mind, body and soul. Tai Chi Chuan, yoga, Qi Gong, Feldenkreis or the vibrational exercises which I have developed are very well suited for this purpose due to their gentle and holistic conception. Walking or moderate, relaxed jogging are also useful. You should avoid: energy-draining, stressful, achievement-oriented and one-sided activities.

Precisely this point should not be underestimated. Frequently this issue is the factor which decides whether or not difficult cases can still be moved in the direction of healing and growth.

4. The more extensively the illness reaches into the psyche, the more the affected person must be involved with the healing and consciously motivated toward change. He or she must become more flexible and want to learn. In many spiritual traditions there is an old maxim: Life energy flows in the direction of conscious or unconscious attention. If the client becomes involved with thoughts of a spiritual, mental or emotional disorder during the Reiki treatment and has the honest desire to constructively heal it and develop his or her existence beyond this dead-end street, Reiki will then be drawn into these physical or energetic areas which have been appealed to in this manner. Then it can effect healing and growth at that point.

5. The more free and lively space existent in the body, mind and soul, the better Reiki can have its effect. More precisely: "If your hands are full, you cannot take hold of anything new!". For the practice of Reiki, this means that other holistic healing systems such as the removal of certain blocks, use of healing stones, aromatherapy, shamanistic purification rituals, relaxing massage or revealing psychotherapy are very helpful in creating the optimal conditions for Reiki to be effective. On the mental level, for example, a great deal of free space can be created in professional and private life by consciously letting go of ideas and opinions that obstruct development or by encouraging a conscious and fair balance of energy in a spiritual sense. It is also important in this respect to release karmic ties through consciously balancing energy, doing exercises to learn how to let go, working on grief and similar tasks.

6. Every healing through Reiki takes place in a natural, holistic manner. On the emotional level, the healing process occurs in three steps:

"Truth"—Healing begins through consciousness. It is usually connected with fear, pain and suffering.

"Love"—The decision to be lively and strive toward unity often brings with it a fluctuating between joy, fulfillment and hope on the one hand and insecurity, relapsing into habits which create separation and support illness and disappointment on the other hand. A more grounded and realistic attitude gradually develops as a result of this.

"Knowledge"—This eventually brings the breakthrough to overall creativity, constructiveness and life-quality improvement by using unconscious aspects of the personality and resources which have previously been scorned or repressed. With this, the healing process is concluded.

A more detailed explanation is probably required on this topic: Before repressed or scorned parts of the personality can be integrated so that a healing occurs on the holistic level, the afflicted person must become conscious of his or her "shadow," as well as becoming aware that there is something within which needs to be healed. In short, he must face his own truth. Every therapy will very quickly reach its limitations if the afflicted individual does not take responsibility for working on his or her own healing, at least within the realm of personal possibilities. The patient then must learn to accept the unaccepted parts within and their messages along with the health problems as a helper, and therefore as an important and correct expression of his or her being. The person must be motivated to appropriately integrate his or her functions and requirements into the life structure, to pay attention to them and to desire to joyfully unite with them in love.

The healing process is complete when the affected person attains a condition of willing, loving acceptance of the hidden talent, the assistance and the potential for more happiness available from his or her shadow and the illness which has resulted, as well as using it creatively and constructively for both personal well-being and that of the surrounding world in a holistic and meaningful manner. The illness, the advice of "develop your self!" has now become superfluous. On the physical level, the well-known phenomenon of *healing reaction* or *an initial change for the worse* and *detoxification* occurs. Exactly this phenomenon illicits a great deal of dismay on the part of both the person conducting the treatment and the person receiving it if the correlations are not understood.

In relation to *detoxification* it should be noted that: If there is too much poison and waste in the body, then the metabolism—in other words, the nourishment, renewal and life-supporting communication of all cells—will be hampered. If the life-obstructing material is eliminated, then this all can function more effectively. However, depending on how much "junk" is in the organism, the healing process can sometimes be very unpleasant. But it is absolutely necessary!

The *initial change for the worse* can also tend to be connected with pain and other accompanying symptoms of suffering like increased vulnerability, listlessness, depression, despondency and the like. Yet, you wanted to become healthy ... This has the following correlation: Illness means there is an energy deficiency in either an organ or an energy center.* A great deal less than what is necessary for healthy liveliness flows in this situation. When something healing is done for this area and it has an effect, more energy is brought to the afflicted area in every case. Now the suffering, the pain, the tension, the weariness, the depression and so forth which have been forced into this area are felt. It is as though you set the dimmer of a lamp to a higher level of illumination. If the lamp only glows dimly, you can see very little in the room. The brighter it becomes, the more clearly you can perceive all the beautiful and ugly things there. However, if a holistic therapy is stopped at a point of the initial change for the worse due to a lack of understanding of the natural healing processes, the opportunity for recovery is also wasted.

However, the further the therapy is continued past the point of the initial change for the worse, the more energy will flow into the blocked areas. The more energy that flows into these blocked places, the deeper the affected areas can recuperate and renew themselves. After all, absolutely nothing happens without energy! At some point the illness-producing pattern or all the disharmonious configurations of this pattern will be eliminated. This occurs in a process of progressive strengthening and healing of the affected areas. This process is dependent on the depth and duration, as well as the strength of the afflicted person's motivation to become truly healthy, with all the consequences for how he or she will live in the future.

---

*This is also true for ailments based on excess energy, because here the effect of that specific energy form which distributes the excess and allows it to flow in a healthy manner is missing!

Then the suffering and overall weakness of the body disappear because it had been forced to direct all reserves towards energizing, purifying and renewing the affected cells, organs and tissue during the healing process. Since many of the bodily functions previously unused due to the illness are now producing energy and performing, a person who has become healthy in a natural way experiences a considerable subjective and objective increase in strength, joy and creativity in all areas.

7. Reiki cannot heal what has been completely destroyed. In such a case, it is only possible to support the bodily functions that can still be stimulated, which have an indirectly positive effect on the total sense of well-being. This means that organs and parts of the body which have died cannot be restored at all or only within the scope of the body's own possibilities for regeneration. In individual cases the effects of congenital deformities and other genetic abnormalities can be greatly assuaged, but it is impossible to completely heal them. On the energetic level this means: If the subtle-energetic double that bears the physical, material structure (in other words, the etheric body) is so strongly disturbed in its vibrations that the healthy areas no longer can fill those which have fallen out of harmony with the life-supportive patterns and regenerate them, because of cancer, for example, then Reiki can no longer heal. In this situation, it can at best dissolve the despair and the feeling of meaninglessness, using creative power to support joy and a feeling of connectedness, thereby providing a gentle and peaceful death.

An understanding of these correlations is important in the following case, as an example: Due to AIDS, a client has suffered through an intensive and meaningful process of learning and growth. He has truly succeeded in achieving a comprehensive understanding of his problems and working through them so that, from a human standpoint, there appears to be no further reason for the illness. Nevertheless, he dies. His etheric structure has been too severly damaged by the strain of the illness to be able to regenerate again. Only those who accept rebirth, life after death and the human being's spiritual task of learning on this level can also fully appreciate how important it is to accompany a dying person in a holistic sense. In the process, Reiki can have many good effects.

Reiki functions in accordance with these seven fundamental laws. In concluding this topic, I would like to expressly emphasize again that Reiki *never* causes disharmonies and/or illness. There are exceptions where a few of the applications may involve a certain risk; however, this risk is based on the interaction between Reiki and other factors (such as chemical medicine which is recognized by the body to be poisonous), but never because of Reiki itself. Reiki is ultimately life and love. There is no overdose of these qualities. However, I must admit that many people who are in the greatest need of love and life sometimes have an intense fear of becoming livelier and more loving. Accordingly, their initial reaction to Reiki is defensive.

Whole-Body Treatment

Reiki's greatest method is the treatment of the whole body. The associated positions are illustrated on pages 20 and 21. The following is fundamentally applicable:

> *By acute and specific complaints (wounds, bruises, etc.) give treatment at the site of the symptom. For chronic complaints, those which effect broad areas of the body or complaints with a psychological background, whole-body treatment should be applied on a regular basis.*

The shortened whole-body treatments presented in this book should be approximately equated with the long form of whole-body treatment for the respective health disorders. Only when the special, shortened whole-body treatment has no effect should the long form also be used—at least alternately— in order to provide an optimal opportunity for healing. Each position of the whole-body treatment should be given at least three minutes of Reiki. It doesn't hurt to do it longer!

Special Positions

Within the scope of the Reiki healing system, special positions* is the term I give to those areas of the body which, when treated directly or through reflex zones, are particularly effective in guiding Reiki to a certain disharmony. Special positions are usually employed after a long or shortened whole-body treatment. Between sessions it is also helpful in most cases to treat them as often as possible.

In contrast to the positions of whole-body treatment, the special positions are applied considerably longer, usually 10 to 20 minutes. They are most effective when employed in connection with the whole-body treatment and are generally not suitable as sole treatment for chronic or deep-seated health disorders. In such cases, the best method to choose is a form of the whole-body treatment, as mentioned above, possibly supported with the appropriate special positions. A wide range of special positions are alphabetically listed and described according to related symptoms in my book "The Complete Reiki Handbook." Those who would like to study this topic in greater detail will find an abundance of material there.

---

*Further explanations can be found in my book "The Complete Reiki Handbook," Lotus Light/Shangri-La

Medication

Reiki stimulates the metabolism and thereby the body's detoxification functions. This basically desirable effect can create problems in certain cases, although these are usually of an insignificant nature.

For this reason, it is important to clarify whether a medication currently being taken must absolutely be kept at a particular concentration in the blood to avoid life-threatening results or severe damage if reduced more quickly than expected (for example, by the liver and kidneys when they have been strengthened by Reiki).

This question can and should only be answered by the attending physician. It is best for the Reiki practitioner to work together and coordinate with him or her. If the doctor knows that the patient's body is functioning better and therefore better able to excrete poisons, the medication can be adjusted accordingly. No danger can occur when this is done.

With time, the body of affected person will become more sensitive and healthier because of Reiki, therefore responding to a lower dosage of medication. The attending physician—and only the attending physician!—can consequently adjust the dosage to the patient's progressing state of health. The reduced strain provided by the lower dosage relieves the patient and contributes to recovery. Medication that works mainly on the energetic level, as in Bach flower essences, homeopathy starting at about 6x, spagyric remedies and similar methods are all supported and intensified in their effects by Reiki.*

Please observe: Reiki never leads to a disharmonious interaction with medication. Only within the scope of an increased detoxification and the associated lessened effect of a medica-

---

*More detailed and extensive information on this important topic can be found in the chapter "Reiki and Medication" in my book "The Complete Reiki Handbook", Lotus Light/Shangri-La

Whole-Body Treatment

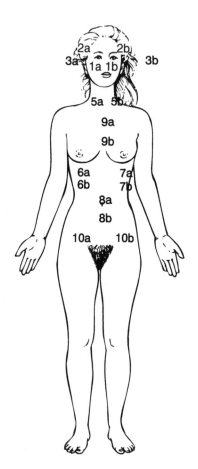

Positions: 1a,b) Forehead to teeth, parallel to the nose; 2a,b,) temples, from the cheekbone beginning in an upward direction; 3a,b) ears; 4) back of the head; 5a,b) front side of neck (do not lay on hands); 6a,b) liver, gallbladder; 7a,b) spleen, pancreas; 8a,b) one hand above and one hand below the navel; 9a,b) thymus gland, heart; 10a,b) pelvic-V (the hands are each

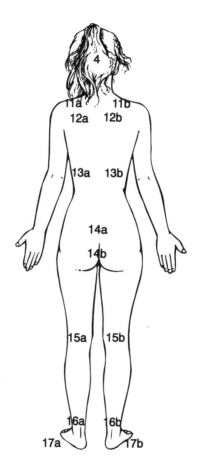

placed on the ridges of the pelvic bones, the tips of the hands close to each other at the pubic bone forming a "V"); 11a,b) between shoulder blades and shoulder; 12a,b) shoulder blades; 13a,b) kidneys; 14a,b) sacrum, under the coccyx to the perineum; 15a,b) hollows of the knees; 16a,b) grasp the ankles; 17a,b) soles of the feet, toes to middle of the foot.

tion should the attending physician pay attention to this situation!

For **diabetics** who take insulin, the following should also be observed: When the Reiki treatment takes effect and the insulin-producing areas of the pancreas begin to work again, it is possible that additional external insulin intake through tablets or injections may create a level of this active agent which is too high, possibly causing severe disturbances.

The attending physician must be informed that the patient's pancreas may have regenerated so that the correct preventive measures can be prescribed. For youthful diabetics, a regeneration of the pancreas seldom occurs since it has been basically destroyed in this region. For elderly diabetics, it is often possible to effect regeneration to different degrees through Reiki treatment which is on a regular basis and appropriately coordinated. The attending physician must be particularly on the alert in this case!

What Else Should I Take into Consideration When Applying Reiki?

The application of Reiki is almost foolproof, even when it is done by lay persons. Nevertheless, two points should be taken into consideration, even though they very rarely lead to disharmonious reactions in the practice.

1. The *spine* should not be *directly* treated in the area starting above the sacrum and extending to directly below the prominent neck vertebrae at the base of the neck. This means: the hands should not cover these spots for a *longer period of time* (which means not more than a few minutes), not *on a regular basis* and not with the *intention of treating them with Reiki*. A variety of subtle-body receptors are located in this section of the spine; they register when the power of love is

represented strongly enough in a number of the main chakras to send the Kundalini energy, a very strong form of polar life energy, from the root chakra where it is concentrated, into the entire body. Reiki *is* love-life energy—however, it comes from the outside. Drawn into the wrong place, it can lead to a false report and permit the Kundalini rise under certain, rare circumstances. Since, among other things, serious physical and psychological problems can occur as a result, these areas should not be provided with Reiki under the stated conditions. There are many other, very effective and safe possibilities for harmonizing spinal problems, such as the ones described in my *Complete Reiki Handbook*.

2. Furthermore, *very weak* people should first be treated with short Reiki treatments (around 5 to 10 minutes, depending on the reaction). This should be done through the soles of the feet and other methods to be decided by the attending physician or healing practitioner, so that the patient becomes stronger and is better able to overcome the stress of a healing reaction without greater difficulties. Every healing method based on natural principles causes a more or less pronounced initial change for the worse and strength-draining detoxification reactions until health is restored. The attending physician must also be informed in this case and you should strive for a close working relationship with him or her!

Chapter 2

Nutrition and Reiki

The last chapter has already made you more familiar with certain laws for the treatment with Reiki.

In this chapter I would like to show how Reiki and nutrition can be optimally combined with each other in the practice.

Dr. Chujiro Hayashi, the second modern Reiki Grand Master, already allowed for special diets harmonizing with the therapies in his clinic. Hawayo Takata, a woman who was his student and the next Grand Master, attached great importance to them as well.

How can this type of diet be developed? And how can someone who has not spent many years examining the various theories of nutrition do this correctly for the benefit of the afflicted person? Within the scope of this presentation, it is naturally not possible to convey everything that a holistic nutritional advisor actually needs to know. However, in many cases this is also not necessary in order to correct major errors in a person's nutritional planning. In case of doubt and when a severe illness exists, a qualified nutritional advisor should obviously be consulted. I would now like to make a few suggestions for home remedies:

Twelve Rules for the Optimal Combination of Food and Reiki Application for Healing

1. Every diet is only good for the time of healing. The diet becomes superfluous, and in fact often harmful, when the healing process has been concluded!

2. The diet should not be put together according to fixed, dogmatic rules, but rather with the needs of the afflicted person in mind, and should be accordingly changed during the course of the illness.

3. At the beginning of a healing process it is often necessary to disrupt certain vicious circles* within the nutrition because these could potentially make recovery more difficult:

    a) the vicious circle of salt
    b) the vicious circle of sugar
    c) the vicious circle of coffee
    d) the vicious circle of alcohol
    e) the vicious circle of protein.

Of course there are other vicious circles in nutrition, but to consider them within this context would take us too far afield. For healing of illness with the methods of "Reiki For First Aid" they are substantially less important.

The vicious circle of salt: This naturally indicates a chronic excessive level of salt consumption. One takes too much salt or automatically chooses dishes with a very high salt content.

---

*Referred to as vicious circles because the particular substance provides no real nourishment, is not appropriate or is already amply available in the body. A further supply strains the organism but is still desired for emotional reasons. Only when the addictive component is disrupted can the body return to a more natural, healthier appetite.

This frequently obstructs the metabolism and detoxification of the tissue. Within the context of these home remedies, this circle can be easily broken. Eat *only watermelon* for two days (but no longer, so that no deficiencies are created). You can eat as much as you want—the more, the better. It contains natural active agents which assist in the elimination of salt deposits, and the lively fruit water supports the removal of waste matter. You will very quickly notice that it is working because you will get a salty taste in your mouth, which can be traced back to the more intensive elimination of salt. Please drink mainly water, preferably without carbonation and with only small quantities of sodium. In addition, small amounts (one to two cups) of black coffee, tea, maté or melissa tea can also be used, naturally without milk, sugar or any type of sweetener. According to my information, these complicate the metabolic function in many cases.

For whom is this important? For all those who frequently dine at cafeterias and restaurants, those who eat large quantities of cheese, meat, chips, french fries, and pickled vegetables and those who strongly salt their foods.

The vicious circle of sugar: The excessive consumption of sugar and white-flour products can be understood as the vicious circle of sugar. In the first place, it strains the pancreas and, secondly, it complicates many of the metabolic functions. It can be broken by a one-to-three-day diet of nothing but grapes (the length depends on the intensity of the craving for sugar).

Beware: This application is not for diabetics!*

Grapes contain active agents which help to secrete sugar. Use the same drinks as in a). For an extensive period of time after-

---

*Diabetics can be cured from the craving for sweets easily, permanently and without risks through a homeopathic cure or by way of the Bach flower essences. Many other problems will often also improve in the process. However, such a cure should be conducted by a doctor of homeopathy or a properly trained healing practitioner. Addresses can be found in the yellow pages.

wards, eat only high-quality, unrefined sweets and stay away from all white-flour products whenever you have an appetite for sweets. This will prevent the vicious circle from being revived.

For whom is this important? For all those who like to consume sugar, sweets, soft drinks, white-flour products and sugar-flavored food on a regular basis. Let yourself be informed by the consumer-advice center in your area as to which foods and treats have sugar in them and how many different terms are used to hide it in convenience foods. You are in for a shock!

The vicious circle of coffee strains many areas of the metabolism, the digestion, the urological system and, above all, the nervous system. There are substantially more coffee and black-tea addicts than you can possibly imagine.

Here's how to free yourself of this addiction: First switch from regular coffee to coffee which has been organically grown for a period of about three weeks and prepare it in a different manner. Instead of the generally popular filter method, use more coarsely ground coffee powder and pour water which has boiled and then cooled directly over it into the pot. A strainer will keep the grinds out of your cup. Coffee prepared in this manner is considerably more digestible and can be enjoyed in small amounts. In fact, it may even increase the feeling of well-being since it actually stimulates digestion. In times past, coffee prepared in this manner was used as an effective medicine against a variety of ailments.

If you are not addicted to coffee, this method of preparation coupled with conscious use is an important tool that will protect you effectively against an addiction to coffee. Then switch over to using organically grown, which means unsprayed, black tea for about three weeks. Afterwards, continue for about three weeks with green tea, which should also be from ecological-organic cultivation.

In conclusion, drink ginger tea for the same amount of time. For this purpose, buy dried ginger root from the herb or health-food store, or, when in doubt, from the pharmacy. For one liter of tea, shave a good pinch of ginger from the root. Brew this powder in water that has boiled and been cooled for three minutes. The three-minute cooling time helps better preserve important active agents. All teas should fundamentally be prepared in this manner.

During this transition period, be sure to get enough vitamin C, E, B-complex, potassium (for example, in the form of bananas, sesame and yeast flakes) and lecithin. Throughout the entire "cure," you should drink one to two cups of melissa tea before going to bed. It is best to use fresh leaves and prepare it in the same manner as the ginger tea. Many symptoms like sleep disturbances, irritation, nervousness, weak concentration, blood pressure which is too high or too low, excessive aggression, daytime tiredness and stomach irritation will disappear or weaken as a result of this change alone.

For whom is this important? For all those who drink coffee or black tea regularly, using it to "wake up" in the morning and "push" during the day.

The vicious circle of alcohol can be healed in milder cases through healthy, high-quality nutrition and the interruption of the vicious circles of sugar and protein. If the afflicted person cannot discontinue alcohol consumption within a period of six weeks through the nutritional changes and efforts of the will, the possibility of addiction may need to be clarified with the help of specialists. A homeopathic cure coupled with psychotherapy has worked true wonders in many such cases. Accusations, putting the blame on someone and an attitude of "I can handle this without help and love heals all" do not accomplish anything and only make the problem worse. Reiki sessions on a regular, at best daily basis, if possible with mental healings with 2nd degree Reiki and selected suggestions, as well as appropriate nutrition, will always contribute to a faster and longer-lasting success of the other measures.*

---

*Alcoholics Anonymous and other self-help organizations are available in almost every city today.

The vicious circle of protein leads to excess waste materials and overly-acidic body tissue because of consuming too much protein on a regular basis. This in turn damages the metabolism and promotes or causes many types of illness. This circle can be broken by starting a day solely with pineapple (caution: only use ripe fruit since unripe fruit can irritate the mouth and stomach! Your local dealer can advise you and supply suitable fruit). The next day, eat only mango or kiwi or apple (always with seeds and skin since they have the largest amount of active agents). Afterwards, you should have a pineapple or a strawberry day every ten days. Between the applications, do not eat meat, cheese or milk. Fish and fowl are permitted in small quantities, as well as small amounts of yogurt, kefir and products from soya which has been produced organically. Do not use any additional salt or salt substitute to spice foods. Instead, use a great deal of fresh herbs. Your diet should mainly consist of fruit, vegetables and grains. This application is also beneficial for your figure and helps get rid of extra pounds in a natural way. Once a year, this "cure" can be carried out for one to two months to great advantage. Please pick stress-free times and use Reiki on a regular basis.

For whom is this important? For all those who regularly eat a great deal of meat, milk products that are not made from raw milk or fish, shellfish and fowl in large quantities.

4. In every diet, attention should be paid to an adequate intake of fluids. Please do not drink liquids during the meals, but rather ten minutes before or two to three hours after eating. This helps the digestion; in this manner, many metabolic and digestive disturbances can even be lessened or healed over the medium term. One-and-a-half to two liters of water is enough fluid consumption for an adult. The water should be as free or as low in carbonation as possible. Those who consume fruit and/or vegetables containing water on a regular basis can manage with one-third to one-half of this amount of

water. Coffee, black tea, beer, herb and fruit teas and fruit and vegetable juices are basically luxury items and not suitable for the direct supply of fluid to the body. The water should come from a good source. City water cannot necessarily be recommended today for a whole variety of reasons. In contrast, water that has been levitated, magnetized or brought into a life-supportive state in other ways is excellently suited. Distilled or demineralized water has been proved to be dangerous to health; therefore, you shouldn't drink it or give it to pets to drink either. After researching the whole topic thoroughly, I believe that only one reason remains for this modern trend of recommending distilled water: it is being pushed for commercial purposes by a few groups that want to sell the not entirely inexpensive water-treatment machines to people. Those who desire to have high-quality nutrition should reflect on the parallels between industrial sugar, refined flour and distilled water. Then the decision is very simple.

5. It is best to only eat in a relaxed or cheerful mood. Eating consciously, not too hastily, chewing well* and enjoying yourself is half of the digestion process, even for the healthy!

6. Thank all those who have contributed to the meal before you eat. Respect the food and do not waste it. The being, whether animal or plant, which gave its life on this level so that your own can be maintained and supported, deserves respect and esteem. It is an expression of spiritual growth to become conscious of these correlations for a moment before each meal, without false feelings of guilt. Primitive peoples have had this loving attitude as a tradition for thousands of

---

*Two important factors are promoted by long chewing: through the extended breaking down of the food into small pieces and salivation, the digestion and assimilation process are enormously supported. A dynamic increase in the effort of the food's subtle patterns takes place in the sense of a homeopathic potentizing which lets the healing powers in it become effective.

years. You will quickly sense that it helps you as well—whether you are healthy or sick!

7. Eating exclusively or primarily raw foods is not for people with greatly weakened vitality or serious digestive problems. This is frequently portrayed to be otherwise, but it is false. Raw foods (which have been organically cultivated) contain a large amount of vital substances requiring a well-functioning digestive system. Only then can the body absorb them and assimilate them in the metabolism. With the precondition of a digestion that is thoroughly healthy, nourishment with raw foods does a great deal of good for body and soul when they are used prudently, undogmatically and in a well-informed manner. Otherwise, they can even do harm! There are frequently so many harmful substances contained in raw foods that have not been grown in organic cultivation that they are more likely to poison than detoxify the organism. By cooking or steaming the food, these poisons primarily go into the water, and the food is cleansed of them for the most part.

8. Cheese, meat and other protein-rich meals should not be eaten together with citrus fruits or juices. These fruits contain active agents that can obstruct protein digestion in people who have been weakened. In addition, when you are sick you should not consume different kinds of fruit at the same time since this could cause digestive disturbances.

9. During the time that Reiki is applied alone or with other therapies to heal severe health disorders, the following foods should be avoided after the vicious circles described above have been harmonized: meat, fish and fowl of all kinds; pasteurized, homogenized, non-fat and highly-heated milk products. Raw milk products, especially yogurt and kefir with a lactic acid content which predominantly turns clockwise are permitted and generally support the healing process. Please avoid alcohol, refined sugar, white-flour products, salt, coffee and black tea.

Note: Reiki often heals when you eat foods which obstruct healing, but this happens more frequently, quickly and intensely when you dispense with them until you are healed. Perhaps your craving for them will also be reduced afterwards.

10. Sprouts can deliver many vitamins, minerals and enzymes in an easily usable and concentrated, natural form. They can be more readily digested than fruit and vegetables and are very tasty. You can raise them at home on the window-sill during the winter. Enjoyed regularly, they are valuable for every healing process and for the maintenance of vitality and health.

11. With Reiki, healthy foods become even healthier and the less healthy ones at least have their value increased! Three to five minutes of Reiki before serving the food, depending on the quantity, makes a huge difference! If you are initiated into the 2nd degree, along with the energy-strengthening of the meal you can also charge it with more vital energy. If the meal has not been prepared in this manner, you can at least turn your hands toward the meal for one or two minutes, either over or next to your plate, and allow Reiki to be drawn in. Drinks, candy and the like can also be made healthier in this manner. When alcohol has been treated like this, it has quite a different taste and has a different effect. Try it out! In my seminars, I often show the participants the healing effect of Reiki on food. With the kinesiological arm test (through the relative strength of a muscle it shows the quality of a particular food) I prove, for example, just how much something like a peppermint bonbon weakens the human energy system. Then the bonbon is treated with Reiki and—lo and behold!—suddenly it no longer weakens the test person! The same goes for tobacco. In case you smoke, try treating your cigarettes extensively with Reiki and you will be amazed. Although Reiki cannot turn strychnine into fructose, within the realm of the possible, fantastic positive changes will occur when you treat your food with it on a regular basis. Lay your hands on your stomach for a while after eating and let Reiki be drawn in. This promotes a healthy digestion in two ways at the same time: first, you will no longer feel tired after the meal and secondly, the nutrients will be absorbed much better into the metabolism.

12. Eat organically grown foods as much as possible. You will find them at your local health-food store or farmer's market. When used regularly, these products raise the general sense of well-being and ensure that you do not get sick as easily. In addition, you contribute to practical environmental protection with them since these foods are consciously grown in an environment kept in a natural state without chemicals. Because of this, the ground, the air and the water stay healthy—and, as a result, so do the people. You can inform yourself through the recommended literature in the annotated bibliography in the index.

How Should the Healthy Person Eat?

A healthy person should essentially eat food that is diversified, according to his or her own healthy appetite*, in portions that are not too large and primarily, but not necessarily, solely from products that are grown in the area and have been cultivated organically. The diet should be made up of one-third fresh vegetarian foods, such as fruit, vegetables and sprouts; one-third lightly steamed or pan-fried fruit and vegetables; and one-third more extensively prepared forms of food, like whole-grain breads, grain flakes, raw milk or raw-milk products, seitan, pickled vegetables, soya products and the like. Small portions of meat, fish or fowl are not harmful when the person is basically healthy and the meat stems from animals

---

*A healthy appetite begins to function when the above-described vicious circles are broken down and dissolved. Otherwise it doesn't!

which have been raised in a natural and caring manner. However, meat is not necessary when you pay attention to a balanced diet. Pork should be avoided at all costs, even by the healthy. Many studies have shown that it can promote or cause various types of illness.

Special Circumstances ...

There are naturally many of these. With a long list of ailments, it is obvious that there are further points to be taken into consideration. The respective information can be found in the next chapters under the corresponding key word for the illness. In addition, it is worthwhile to learn more about healthy nutrition in any case. Almost every adult evening school offers the appropriate courses for further studies, most likely in your neighborhood as well. Pull yourself together and look into it! You will also find a some very good books on this topic in the annotated bibliography.

Chapter 3

How You Can Work Out Effective Special Positions for Reiki Application

Special positions and whole-body treatments are depicted in many Reiki books. However, to my knowledge, up to now there have been no exact explanations on why specific positions work just as they do and not in another manner. At the same time, this is not difficult to understand and opens up a broad field of activity which someone with a holistic understanding of the reasons can very easily and appropriately fill in with their own creativity.

What Kind of Special Positions are There?

An overview of the different types of positions and effects will contribute to a better understanding of the positions used in the Reiki treatment.

1. Positions with a direct function. This means that the hands are, for example, laid on the body above the liver or held over a specific chakra to cover its energy field. This point can be further divided into:

    1.1. Positions for the material realm, which means the "touchable" body, the acupuncture meridians, rings of muscle armour, energy organs, as well as

    1.2. Positions for the subtle body such as the major and secondary chakras and the fields of the aura.

2. Positions with indirect functions. These are the many

greatly differing reflex zones, through which all the organism's important function carriers, such as the chakras, organs, nerve centers and the like, can be reached. Their effect is sometimes achieved far away from the actual spot. Because of this, it is possible to reach all the main chakras in the best way through the inner sides of the feet. Here we can also differentiate between

2.1 Reflex zones, that are associated with the material realm and

2.2 Reflex zones, that are associated with the subtle realm.

How Do You Determine a Special Position for a Particular Health Disorder?

The first thing to do is fundamentally categorize the symptoms which occur. The following is offered as a basic description of a simplified system that I developed through the years in the course of my practice ...

1. Can it be determined that one or more body areas or organs are in disharmony? Here is an example: Are the stomach or kidneys in pain, does your throat hurt, has your vision worsened, did you cut yourself in the finger or do you have a bruise? In that case, first treat the area where it hurts, which means where the disorder can be localized. In some cases, it is good to get to know the body and its functions a bit better. One example: you determine that you have a strong aversion to fatty foods and can't tolerate alcohol too well. You should understand this as a request from your self to give intensified treatment to the liver and pancreas with Reiki. Both of these organs are namely directly involved in the digestion of fat.

The liver has to detoxify the alcohol, and the pancreas probably has the most sensitive reaction to poisons of all the body's organs. This type of inference can be made more easily than you possibly think at the moment. In the annotated bibliography you will find several books that give helpful instructions to this effect. Study these suggestions, try them out and you will quickly discover that it is really not all that complicated. It is naturally necessary to give it some effort, but this exertion will soon pay off ...

2. Now you can find the reflex zones of the hand, foot and other reflex zones connected to the affected organ and body areas, applying Reiki in addition to treating them on its own. Disorders can frequently be harmonized more easily through reflex zones located farther away from the actual affected area than those directly on it. There is a general rule for this: If you cannot get direct access, choose the reflex zone which is farthest away to continue the treatment. But how will you know where these reflex zones are located? Well, I've saved you some work and researched a little. The results can be found in the annotated bibliography in the index.

3. Now you can, for example, assign to the disorder an acupuncture meridian, specific acupuncture points or a collection of them, the main or secondary chakras, the energy organs and the aura fields; then treat the respective areas directly or with reflexology. This method is recommended especially for types of illness which effect broad areas of the body, as well as chronic and psychological disharmonies, as a supplement to the Reiki treatment. Books that will further help you can also be found on this topic in the annotated bibliography.

4. Another method comes from the development of the subtle senses. If you take the time to develop your abilities of perception in this area, you will be able to sometimes very quickly detect for yourself and others where Reiki would be particularly useful in each special case.

5. If you carefully observe and question people, you will notice that the afflicted have certain bodily areas where they like to lay their hands. They also do this without ever having heard anything about Reiki or any other type of energy work. One example with which everyone is familiar is that pregnant women frequently lay their hands on their backs in the area of the kidneys. The kidneys are actually intensely strained during pregnancy and a certain redistribution of energy in the body is promoted by the laying on of hands. With Reiki, this is substantially more intensive. You only need to pay attention to these natural indications. Ask, for example, where the person most enjoys being touched during a massage or where he or she most frequently puts the hands when laying them on the body during the course of the day. Similar to aura and chakra reading, this method you will teach you an incredible amount about illness, reflex zones and possibilities for healing which you cannot find in any book. So, that's it already! Not too bad, hmm? Now you can get started and discover your own positions.

Chapter 4

Short Treatment and Special Positions

—With a Supplement on Natural-Healing Methods for 44 Ailments and Types of Illness—

Before I introduce the special treatment methods to you, there are still a few instructions necessary for your use.

First, the most important: The methods given here, as previously stated, are not meant to make a visit to the doctor, healing practitioner or psychotherapist superfluous! When in question, you should therefore always seek qualified counsel. Especially in the case of severe illness, the attending physician or therapist should be informed about the use of Reiki.

In each case I have noted where, in my opinion, it is very important to quickly consult a professional. In order to make optimal use of the applications presented here, first try out the appropriate short treatment on three or four consecutive days (unless otherwise indicated). Afterwards, do it at least one to two times a week. In difficult cases, do it every day. If the person still doesn't respond after four days of treatment (pay careful attention to physical and psychological solution, purification and healing processes), switch to a longer whole-body treatment for four days, as described in Chapter 1. Afterwards, you can continue with the short treatment. Healing reactions are always a good sign.

In order to keep them and the associated strain within limits, stretch out the intervals between individual treatments when healing reactions occur. For example, instead of every day, only use the Reiki treatment every three days. It depends greatly on the individual case and the person's frame of mind. In case of doubt in terms of a healing reaction, a naturopath should be consulted. The supplemental natural-healing methods can be applied parallel to Reiki. When there is severe illness, intensive physical weakness and in all cases of doubt, the application of these methods should be discussed with the attending doctor of naturopathy or the healing practitioner because they must be as extensively informed about the case as possible in order to make a proper assessment.

Especially in the case of chronic or psychically-caused illness, a longer period of time may be necessary before there are clear signs of improvement. The key to success may lie in the necessary patience here.

More intensive information about Reiki treatment, healing and the like can be found in the books which I have presented in the annotated bibliography in the index.

When I give tips about *healing foods* and *herbs*, I always assume that those used are organically grown, such as those which you will find at certain farmer's markets and natural-food stores. They should be fresh, which means not having been subjected to long storage periods before use. *Honey* should be cold-strained, in a natural state and from ecologically kept bees, if at all possible. If honey is heated, it loses its entire effectiveness. Therefore, never put it into foods that are warmer than body temperature. Please handle herbs in the same manner. *Herbs*, as well as *garlic* and *onions*, should be cut directly before consumption. I often recommend garlic because it has a healing power which in many cases is undefeatable. It should be eaten on a regular basis, but not in large quantities and preferably together with other foods. Some people are disturbed by the smell. In order to avoid this problem, chew well on a coffee bean or some fresh parsley after eating garlic. A few bites of banana or some milk can also help.

People who are sick should not eat anything that has been

reheated. The healthy should not make it a habit either. Food that has been repeatedly reheated is suitable for neither the healthy nor the sick.

Note: If the sick person has a strong dislike for a particular healing food or medicine, it should be discontinued. He or she should be given a different remedy with the appropriate effective spectrum and food that stimulates the appetite.

A tip from shamanistic healing: Take healing herbs, medicine and healing foods in your hands or hold your hands over them and direct your attention to the heart area. Then ask the Creative Force and the spirit/angel of the plants for their blessing and their assistance in the healing. Thank Mother Earth and Father Sun for their gifts that let us live and give us healing. Spend a moment in this consciousness, and sense how the radiant power of the remedies treated in this manner spreads.

In the following text, I describe in detail three Reiki applications for the 2nd degree that are frequently very useful. Later I will only refer to them by the key word.

I. Mental Healing with Affirmation

From one of the books on the topic of "affirmations" by Louise Hay or Shakti Gawain, select a affirmation which you think is suitable for you for Reiki mental healing or combine a number of appropriate affirmations into a pendulum table and then find the right one for you with the pendulum.

Now use the mental healing with Reiki to give treatment every day for three to five minutes at a time, if possible, and constantly repeat the selected affirmation in your mind while doing so.

Attention! The Reiki mental healing is not a suggestive or hypnotic method! Within this context, the affirmation only shows the best holistic way so that Reiki can have an optimal affect.

In the following chapters of this book, I refer to this method under the key word "Mental Healing with Affirmation."

II. Reiki Contact with the Inner Child

Take a few minutes to make contact with the *inner child* of the afflicted person on a regular basis, at least two to three times a week.

For this purpose, use absent healing of the 2nd degree by saying: "Inner child of ... (first and last name of the afflicted person)" (repeat three times). This process basically strengthens the recipient of the absent healing's will for life, vitality, flexibility and intuition. It is possible that many blocked feelings will be resolved and freed during the course of the treatment.

An environment should be created in which the people treated can experience these energies with someone there to lean on and catch them. Several hours of psychotherapy are very helpful, especially when the inner life is strongly set into motion through the Reiki treatment. I refer to this in the following with the key words "Reiki for the *Inner Child*."

III. Reiki Contact with the Higher Self

Take a few minutes to make contact with the *higher self* of the afflicted person on a regular basis, at least two to three times a week. For this purpose, use absent healing of the 2nd degree with by saying: "*Higher self* of ... (first and last name of the afflicted person)" (repeat three times). This method strengthens the ties of the affected person with his or her spiritual path; as a result, he or she can better (and more deeply) tune in to the lessons that need to be unravelled. If the afflicted person is willing, the *higher self* can more easily help them to become healthy in this manner. In addition to this, the *higher self* can lead the sick person to an understanding of the ailment's message, accept it and integrate it into his or her own being. New paths can open up that lead to happiness and joy, success and growth for the afflicted person. I refer to this method in the following text with the key words "Reiki for the *higher self.*"

I have dispensed with describing the "normal" first-aid measures since they are well-documented and can be (and should be!) learned through courses which are accessible to everyone. The methods presented here are not meant to replace, but rather to meaningfully enrich these measures. Note: The treatment sequences for Reiki 1 should be carried out in the order indicated by the numbers. Terms like 1a and 1b mean that one hand treats position 1a) while the other is on position 1b) at the same time. Terms like 1a), 1b), 1c) mean that one hand treats position 1a), while the other provides 1b) with Reiki at the same time. Then change the hand from 1b) to 1c), while the other remains on 1a).

Applications

Acne

General: Acne is a disorder of the sebaceous glands. The basis is frequently an innately oily skin (seborrhea) with strong hornification. Inflammations are provoked through the influence of bacteria. Causes for the increased production of fat can be assumed to be stress, being overworked and emotional and psychological factors. Acne usually appears most intensely during puberty because the skin, as a relationship and contact organ, is connected to the sexual glands and the second chakra, which assume their functions at this time. Be careful! Some medications trigger acne. Allergies can also be responsible. Acne is a complex illness that should be treated holistically and always has a psychological background unless it is a reaction brought on by medicine.

Reiki treatment with 1st degree: Give the following positions for at least five minutes each on a long-term basis—

1a) forehead and 1b) back of the head; 2a,b) shoulder blades; 3) solar plexus; 4) lower abdomen; 5a,b) kidneys; 6) sacrum.

Reiki treatment with 2nd degree: Mental healing with affirmations; in severe cases, use Reiki for the *inner child.*

Natural-healing supplement: Eat a finely minced raw garlic clove in any form, even divided up into portions, every day. Use the kombucha and the wheat-grass juice* (2-3 tbsp. of juice 3 times a day) on a regular basis. Every morning before breakfast, drink a glass of water that is not too cold, stirring in a good teaspoon of cold-strained honey from ecologically kept bees. Use many unsaturated fatty acids which are found in thistle oil, margarine from the health-food store and the like. A vegetarian diet is best, but pork should be eliminated from the diet in any case. Be sure to get enough vitamins, especially the B-complex, A and E. Add fresh or dried thyme to every meal. Apply masks of healing earth on the affected areas regu-

---

*Or any other drink containing chlorophyll, such as "Kyo-Green" (see suppliers on page 153).

Acne

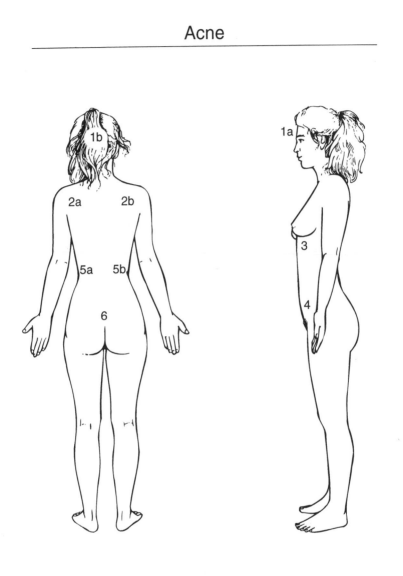

Treatment positions:

1a) Forehead and 1b) back of the head; 2a,b) shoulder blades;
3) solar plexus; 4) lower abdomen; 5a,b) kidneys; 6) sacrum.

larly. Use a neutral medicinal soap. Dispense with all decorative, non-medicinal cosmetics.

Visit to a doctor/healing practitioner: This is only necessary in stubborn cases.

Visit to a psychotherapist: It can very much help in difficult and stubborn cases since existing psychological problems can be discovered and harmonized, making a lasting cure possible for the first time in difficult cases!

Allergies

General: The allergy can be a perfectly appropriate defensive reaction against substances which the body does not tolerate for a whole variety of reasons. The body builds special antibodies against these "allergies," which are unnoticed at first. The allergic person has now become sensitized to these foreign substances. When a renewed contact with the same substance occurs, the body reacts with a defensive response. We are still largely in the dark as to why a person reacts allergically to a particular substance. Certain forms of allergies are hereditary and others are acquired during the course of life. From the perspective of spiritual healing, the substance that causes the allergy is seen as a symbol for something that the afflicted person does not want to embody with his or her own being. This repressed part can be lovingly integrated so that the allergy becomes superfluous, which usually requires a great deal of patience and qualified assistance.

Reiki treatment with 1st degree: For at least six weeks, give the following positions for at least four minutes each every day on a long-term basis —1a) forehead with third eye, 1b) back of head with medulla oblongata; 2a,b) ears; 3) skull cap; 4) solar plexus to the navel; 5a,b) pelvic V; 6) sacrum; 7a,b) kidneys; 8a,b) soles of the feet.

Reiki treatment with 2nd degree: Mental treatment with suggestions.

Natural-healing supplement: Take the Swedish Bitters™*, silicea balsam and the kombucha for a longer period of time. Switch to vegetarian nutrition.

Visit to a doctor/healing practitioner: This should always take place in difficult and stubborn cases.

Visit to a psychotherapist: This is very helpful in stubborn and difficult cases.

---

*Do not use during pregnancy because of its camphor content.

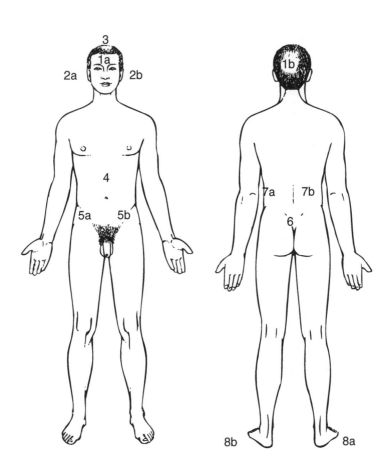

Treatment positions:

1a) Forehead with third eye, 1b) back of head with medulla oblongata; 2a,b) ears; 3) skull cap; 4) solar plexus to the navel; 5a,b) pelvic V; 6) sacrum; 7a,b) kidneys; 8a,b) soles of the feet.

Bleeding

General: Bleeding, except in the case of bleeders, does not actually represent an independent illness. For information on hemorrhoidal bleeding, look under "Hemorrhoids." Nose-+bleeding can be a detoxification measure by the body for the head area. When this tendency exists, an experienced naturopath should carry out an examination. Blood in the stools, the urine or in secretions which have been coughed up should definitely be examined by a doctor in all cases! Also see "Wounds."

Reiki treatment with 1st degree: For wounds, give Reiki directly above them, but always without skin contact. Do this until the bleeding stops, which usually occurs very quickly. For the treatment of nosebleeds and tendencies toward nosebleeding, give the following positions for at least six minutes—1a) lay one hand on the nose and 1b) one hand on the back of the head; 2a) above the throat (without contact) and 2b) on the nape of the neck. For long-term treatment of bleeders and people whose blood does not clot as well as it should, give the following positions for a longer period of time—1b,c) back of the head and forehead; 2a,b); 3a) solar plexus, 3b) heart chakra; 4a) sacrum, 4b) from beneath the coccyx to the perineum; 5a,b) on the soles of the feet from the toes to at least the middle of the foot.

Reiki treatment with 2nd degree: Mental treatment with suggestions; for bleeders, definitely also do Reiki for the *inner child* and the *higher self.*

Natural-healing supplement: In case normal first-aid measures are not successful or unnecessary and a doctor has not yet arrived, the following can be tried: mashed garlic laid on the wound promotes blood clotting and disinfects at the same time. A similar effect can be obtained from salt mixed with flour, black tea crumbs and also lemon juice. It hurts, but is better than an even greater loss of blood. Nettle tea helps weaken

Bleeding

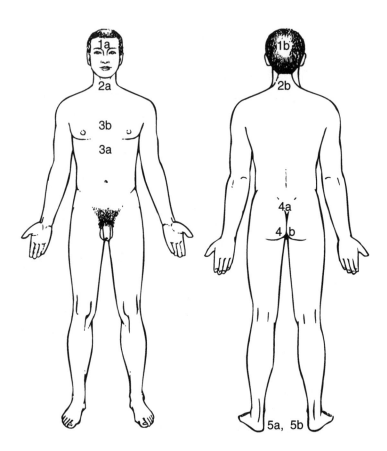

Treatment positions:

1a) One hand on the forehead and third eye, 1b) one hand on the back of the head; 2a) above the throat (without contact) and 2b) on the neck; 3a) solar plexus, 3b) heart chakra; 4a) sacrum, 4b) coccyx to the perineum; 5a,b) soles of the feet from the toes to the middle of the foot.

menstrual bleeding which is too strong. After an intensive loss of blood, horsetail tea with plenty of natural honey should be taken for a time, in an amount of at least about three cups a day. When larger blood vessels (arteries, etc.) are injured, the most important thing is naturally first-aid with the application of a tourniquet and compression bandage. You can learn more about this subject in a first-aid class.

Visit to a doctor/healing practitioner: In cases of strong bleeding and injuries to bleeders: go immediately to the emergency room!

Visit to a psychotherapist: This is generally not necessary.

Blood Pressure (Too High/Too Low)

General: Today stronger and longer-lasting deviations in blood pressure appear in people with increasing frequency, even during the younger years. These problems are often symptoms accompanying other types of organic or emotional illness, a situation which must absolutely be clarified.

Reiki treatment with 1st degree: Give the following positions on a long-term basis—1a) forehead with third eye, 1b) back of head with medulla oblongata, 2a,b) with both hands touching the nape of the neck, clasp the throat at the sides; 3a,b) one hand in front of the throat, the other on the nape of the neck; 4) solar plexus; 5a,b) kidneys; 6a,b) soles of the feet from the toes to at the middle of the foot. For excessive high blood pressure and congestion of blood in the head region, **do not** treat this area, but instead only do 4) and, above all, 6a,b).

Reiki treatment with 2nd degree: Mental treatment with suggestions.

Natural-healing supplement: For blood pressure which is too high or too low: Drink a large glass of fresh white-cabbage juice (for preparation, see "Detoxification;" for excessively high blood pressure, prepare *without* wheat-germ oil, for low blood pressure prepare *with* wheat-germ oil) every day in the morning and evening. Eat a lettuce salad which as fresh as possible every day. For the medium term, exercise on a regular basis is helpful for blood pressure which is too low. Also drink rosemary tea. For raised blood pressure: daily one or two garlic cloves, finely minced and divided into portions to be taken with meals. Always use fresh garlic and don't heat it! Eat pumpkin and squash on a regular basis.

Visit to a doctor/healing practitioner: This should absolutely take place! Definitely discuss home remedies and have their effects checked on a regular basis.

Visit to a psychotherapist: This is useful when no organic causes can be determined or when the illness doesn't respond well to the therapy.

Blood Pressure (Too High/Too Low)

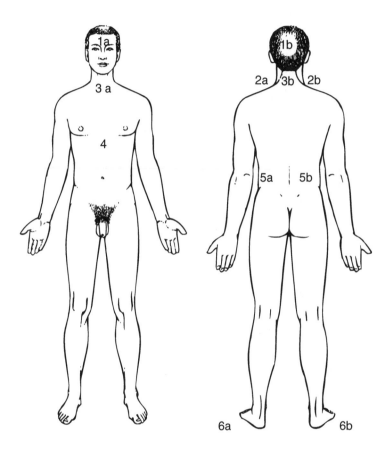

Treatment positions:

1a) Forehead with third eye, 1b) back of head with medulla oblongata; 2a,b) both sides of the nape of the neck; 3a,b) one hand in front of the throat, the other on the nape on the neck; 4) solar plexus; 5a,b) kidneys; 6a,b) soles of the feet from the toes to the middle of the foot.

Broken Bones

General: The treatment of broken bones naturally belongs in the hands of a doctor. However, home remedies can help speed up an uncomplicated healing process. In energetic terms, the first main chakra is responsible here.

Reiki treatment with 1st degree: Treat directly at the site of the fracture several times daily for at least fifteen minutes at a time. In addition, give Reiki on the sacrum and from beneath the coccyx to the perineum, at least five minutes at a time. The more frequently, the better the results will be!

Reiki treatment with 2nd degree: Mental healing with affirmations and in case of extensive fractures, also give Reiki for the *inner child* and the *higher self.*

Natural-healing supplement: Homeopathic remedy: fifteen drops of Symphytum 2x three times daily; two tablets of Arnica 6x two times daily as well as two tablets of Calcium Phosphoricum 6x two times daily until it has healed.

Visit to the doctor/healing practitioner: It is essential that the injured person immediately goes to the doctor! It is best to go to a specialist for sports or accident injuries since some general practitioners don't have a complete enough understanding to interpret x-rays for complicated breaks, in the foot or hand area, for example. In the case of presumed bruises or sprains, be sure to clarify whether it is not actually a break.

Visit to a psychotherapist: Not useful, except when there is a pronounced tendency toward injury.

Bronchial Asthma

General: Bronchial asthma is a severe illness. It requires a specialized medical examination and diagnosis. The lay person cannot possibly determine whether it is really bronchial asthma or another illness in a particular case. For example, an allergy or cardiac asthma might be concealed behind the symptoms or a medicine has been given which causes symptoms similar to bronchial asthma. Only when bronchial asthma has been definitively diagnosed, should you begin with special therapy under the supervision of a doctor. In most cases, the treatment will take much time, as well as a great deal of patience. It will demand the personal participation of the patient, who must seriously strive for a psycho-physical development away from the disharmony.

Reiki with the 1st degree: During an attack, lay one hand on the solar plexus and the other on the chest. Or treat the chest or solar-plexus region every four to five minutes in rotation with both hands. For the long term, treat the following positions for at least five minutes each every day for at least six weeks—1a) forehead with third eye and 1b) back of the head with the medulla oblongata; 2a,b) ears; 3a,b) shoulder blades; 4) solar plexus; 5) spleen; 6a,b) kidneys. In case of exhaustion after a severe attack—1), 2), 4), 6), and 7) sacrum—six minutes each. Also very effective—with one hand hold onto a thumb and treat the same side of the chest with the other hand. Then do exactly the same with the other thumb and the other side of the chest.

Reiki treatment with 2nd degree: Give Reiki for the *inner child*, the *higher self*, and mental healing with affirmations.

Natural-healing supplement: Eat some radish with a little honey on a regular basis every day. Fresh horseradish is even better, also with honey. Prepared in this way, you will liquefy the congested mucous in the body. Don't add salt because it can prevent the absorption of the active agents from vegeta-

Bronchial Asthma

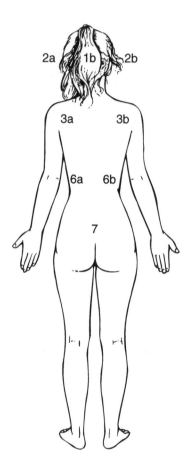
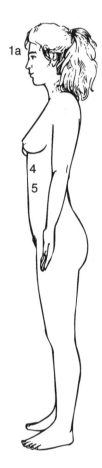

Treatment positions:

1a) Forehead with third eye and 1b) back of head with medulla oblongata; 2a,b) ears; 3a,b) shoulder blades; 4) solar plexus; 5) spleen; 6a,b) kidneys; 7) sacrum.

bles! Eat a great deal of salad made from raw sauerkraut (not pasteurized!) with onions *or* garlic (finely minced). If the liver and gallbladder are not in order, which must first be diagnosed by a physician, garlic and onions may possibly have to be omitted. The consumption of dairy products should be minimized; if at all, then only eat those which have been made from raw milk. The fundamental diet should be vegetarian and low in protein! Avoid refined sugar. Drink plenty of water and, if necessary, keep the respiratory air in the residential space moist with an air humidifier that works on the vaporizer principle. Avoid excitement and stress.

Visit to a doctor/healing practitioner: This must absolutely take place! These attacks can be life-threatening and must be treated with prescription medicine under certain circumstances. A trained homeopathist can see to it that this is replaced by homeopathic medicines in time.

Visit to a psychotherapist: This is recommended since asthma basically has an extensive psychological background!

Burns

General: In the course of daily life, a burn can sometimes quickly happen. The methods described here are for the lighter first-degree burns (reddening and painful skin) and smaller second-degree burns (blistering) and for emergencies when no doctor or hospital can be reached.

Reiki treatment with 1st degree: Treat the affected areas of the skin directly. Don't touch it during treatment! The pain will increase at first, but then quickly subside. Always treat for about ten minutes after the point at which the pain begins to decrease following the initial increase. In cases of larger burns, additionally give the whole-body treatment.

Reiki treatment with 2nd degree: Only in cases of larger burns, give Reiki for the *inner child* on a regular basis along with extended mental treatment with suggestions. In cases of third-degree burns, also give Reiki for the *higher self.*

Natural-healing supplement: Cool immediately with tap water. This is useful for up to sixty minutes after the burn has occurred. Under no circumstances should you use ice, ice-water, something hot or turpentine! Put raw, grated potatoes on the burn. Use a compress with healing earth.

Visit to a doctor/healing practitioner: Burns occur in three degrees. It is absolutely necessary to go to a doctor starting with larger second- degree burns (blistering, accelerated pulse, fever) and in cases of lesser second-degree burns for diabetics and those with cardiac or kidney diseases!

Visit to a psychotherapist: Only appropriate in difficult cases with trauma and possible disfigurement.

General: Many people suffer under chronic exhaustion in our age. There are a variety of reasons for this. Also look under "Detoxification."

Reiki treatment with 1st degree: Give the following positions every day over a longer period of time for at least five minutes each—1a) solar plexus, 1b) liver; 2a,b) pelvic V, lay the hands to form a V from the pelvic bones to the pubic bone; 3a,b) collar-bones; 4a) sacrum, 4b) from beneath the coccyx to the perineum; 5a,b) kidneys; 6a,b) beneath the shoulder from the prominent cervical vertebrae on both sides toward the front; 7a,b) soles of the feet from the tips of the toes to at least the middle of the foot.

Reiki treatment with 2nd degree: Mental treatment with suggestions and Reiki for the *inner child.*

Natural-healing supplement: Live with a vegetarian diet for a longer period of time and eliminate alcohol, black tea and chocolate. Two to three times a day, use the Swedish Bitters™*, kombucha and wheat-grass juice** (2-3 tbsp.). Eat a lettuce salad (as fresh as possible) prepared with apple-cider vinegar, wheat-germ oil, alfalfa sprouts and a garlic clove every day. Drink freshly pressed carrot juice with some wheat-germ oil and lemon juice daily. Regular exercise outdoors and brisk or normal walking is helpful.

Visit to a doctor/healing practitioner: It is essential to consult an experienced naturopath and have an exact diagnosis made in order to uncover any possible form of serious illness in time to give it proper treatment.

Visit to a psychotherapist: Appropriate when no organic causes can be ascertained.

---

*Do not use during pregnancy because of its camphor content.

**Or any other drink containing chlorophyll, such as "Kyo-Green" (see suppliers on page 153).

Chronic Exhaustion

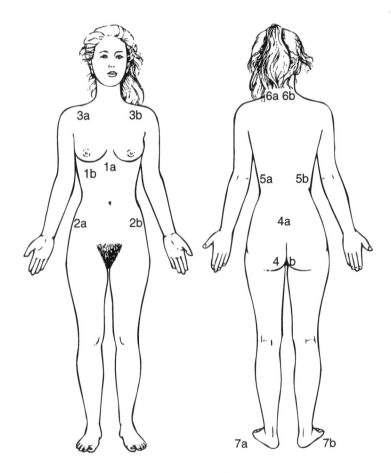

Treatment positions:

1a) Solar plexus, 1b) liver; 2a,b) pelvic V; 3a,b) collar-bones; 4a) sacrum, 4b) from beneath the coccyx to the perineum; 5a,b) kidneys; 6a,b) beneath the shoulder from prominent cervical vertebrae on both sides toward the front; 7a,b) soles of the feet, toe tips to the middle of the foot.

Circulatory Disorders/Legs

General: One possible cause is deficient blood supply to the extremities brought about by atherosclerosis, nicotine misuse, metabolic disorders (diabetes), vascular damage as a result of injury, long-term work in the cold, as a result of intensive and lengthy emotional excitation (spasms), as well as for hereditary reasons. The amount of blood available cannot satisfy the actual daily requirements of the affected area. As a result, insufficient nourishment reaches the tissue and the metabolic waste is adequately removed.

Reiki with 1st degree: Give the following positions every day over a longer period of time for ten minutes each until the person has been completely cured—1) solar plexus; 2a) one hand on the sacrum and with the other 2b,c) treat the underside of the foot, first on one heel and then on the other; 3) then treat the legs, handbreadth by handbreadth, first on the front side and then on the back, from the pelvis all the way down to the feet. Hold each position for at least four minutes.

Attention! If the legs begin to hurt after a few treatments, definitely continue the treatment! This is a sign of stronger circulation and along with it, healing! The pain may become so strong for a while that the use of pain-killer or acupuncture may be necessary.

Reiki treatment with 2nd degree: Mental treatment with suggestions. Reiki for the *inner child.*

Natural-healing supplement: Drink kombucha and wheatgrass juice* (2-3 tbsp. of juice 3 times a day) and a big glass of freshly pressed white-cabbage juice, stirring in a finely minced fresh garlic clove (see preparation under "Detoxification") every day. Add a garlic clove, finely minced, to the kombucha and a second one, finely minced, in portions with meals. In severe cases, greatly increase the amount of garlic eaten. The circula-

---

*Or any other drink containing chlorophyll, such as "Kyo-Green" (see suppliers on page 153).

Circulatory Disorders/Legs

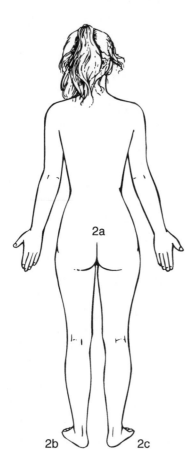
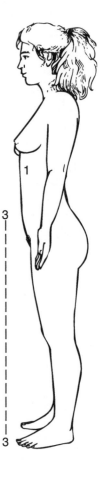

Treatment positions:

1) Solar plexus; 2a) sacrum, 2b,c) undersides of the feet, on the heels, right and left; 3) legs.

tion can be vastly improved in this manner. In addition, eat one ripe pineapple daily. If there are wounds, multi-layered compresses with white-cabbage leaves (use described under "Sore Throat") can help. They should be changed every few hours. Compresses can also be done with healing earth. To intensify the effect of these two types of compresses, apply the Swedish Bitters™* to the wounds. Weight loss is imperative if the person is overweight! Keep the legs raised as much as possible and do exercises designed to stimulate good circulation on a regular basis. Drink plenty of liquids. Eliminate meat and milk products from the diet. Drink plenty of water.

Visit to a doctor/healing practitioner: Must definitely take place since serious complications can arise as a result of untreated or incorrectly diagnosed and falsely treated illness. Other causes like rheumatism, arterial occlusion, thrombosis, etc., must be specifically clarified.

Visit to a psychotherapist: Only appropriate in stubborn cases to eliminate psychological obstacles to recovery.

---

*Do not use during pregnancy because of its camphor content.

Colds

General: Colds happen in the best of families. If they occur two or four times a year for a period of a week, they can simply be the body's detoxification measures. They shouldn't be simply dried out with some sort of nasal spray. These chemical clubs almost always damage the mucous membranes when used regularly. They also impede the detoxification process, which can have very unpleasant results under certain circumstances. Instead, detoxification should be supported and the body's powers of resistance strengthened. Also see "Immune-System Deficiencies" and "Detoxification."

Reiki treatment with 1st degree: Give the following positions several times daily for at least five minutes each until the condition is cured—1a,b) from the forehead to the teeth, parallel to the nose; 2a,b) temples; 3a,b) ears; 4a,b) collar-bones; 5) solar plexus; 6a,b) pelvic V, lay the hands in a V form from the pelvic bones to the pubic bone; 7a,b) soles of the feet from the toe tips to the middle of the foot. In between times, give 1a,b) and 4a,b) frequently.

Reiki treatment with 2nd degree: For a stubborn colds, use mental treatment with suggestions and Reiki for the *inner child.*

Natural-healing supplement: Every morning before breakfast, drink a large glass of kombucha and the juice of one half of a squeezed lemon. Also drink wheat-grass juice* (2-3 tbsp. of juice 3 times a day). If you want, sweeten it with honey. For lunch, eat a grapefruit with a good tablespoon of honey and evenings drink a large glass of fresh cabbage juice (for preparation, see "Detoxification"). Eat at least two finely grated apples (with skin and seeds) with honey and lemon juice every day. To open up the nose, rub the chest with tiger balsam. If you start using these measures at the first signs of a cold, it will

---

*Or any other drink containing chlorophyll, such as "Kyo-Green" (see suppliers on page 153).

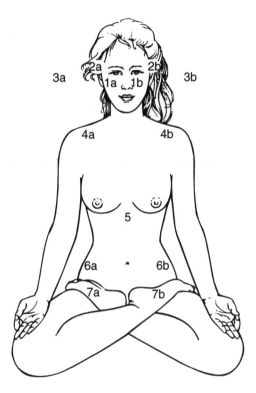

Treatment positions:

1a,b) Forehead to teeth, parallel to the nose; 2a,b) temples; 3a,b) ears; 4a,b) collar-bones; 5) solar plexus; 6a,b) pelvic V; 7a,b) soles of the feet, toe tips to the middle of foot.

rarely actually develop into one. Tenacious mucous can be loosened by sniffing finely grated marjoram.

Visit to a doctor/healing practitioner: If the head cold lasts longer than ten days despite these home remedies or if other symptoms like fever, headache and the like appear, definitely consult a naturopath in order to prevent any possible complications and inflammations of the paranasal sinuses and frontal sinuses. Allergies and the like can then be recognized in time to heal properly them.

Visit to a psychotherapist: Only appropriate for stubborn cases and very long-lasting colds since it is necessary to clarify why the afflicted person always "is sick of things."

Constipation

General: Constipation is usually hereditary or can be traced to faulty lifetime habits. Activities that require much sitting, a lack of movement, unsuitable diet, certain medication and loss of tone in the stomach musculature all contribute to difficulty in excreting the stool. Frequently, a psychological component and/or damaged intestinal flora are also contributing factors.

Reiki with 1st degree: Provide the entire stomach and pelvic region with Reiki. In between times, treat the solar plexus and the lower abdominal region as often as possible.

Reiki treatment with 2nd degree: Mental treatment with suggestions. In severe cases, also Reiki for the *inner child.*

Natural-healing supplement: Drink large amounts of sauerkraut juice or kombucha. Switch to a high-quality vegetarian diet and avoid hot spices. Eat fresh, roughly ground linseed that's been allowed to swell in water or, better yet, in yogurt or kefir and then sweetened with honey on a regular basis. At least two tomatoes should be eaten with every meal— or drink fresh tomato juice. Make sure to get plenty of liquids, for an adult at least one-and-a-half to two quarts a day. Take the Swedish Bitters™* three times a day and eat plenty of kefir and yogurt. Don't eat or drink anything that has peppermint in it! Get stomach massages and make sure you have exercise regularly. Treat all drinks and foods with Reiki.

Visit to a doctor/healing practitioner: For constipation which occurs on a regular basis or is long-lasting (more than three days), an experienced naturopath should absolutely be consulted since constipation can be a symptom of other types of illness and can strain the body if it continues for a longer period of time.

Visit to a psychotherapist: If there are no organic causes to be found and the usual healing methods don't work, a psychotherapy can be of great help.

---

*Do not use during pregnancy because of its camphor content.

Cough

General: Coughing can occur on its own, but may also be an accompanying symptom of another illness. Most of the time, other cold symptoms such as sore throat, hoarseness, flu, fever and the like appear as well. If this is the case, please also look under the individual key words.

Reiki treatment with 1st degree: Give the following positions several times a day for about ten minutes each—1a,b) collar-bones; 2a,b) middle of chest. Additionally only in severe cases: 3a,b) take the hands of the afflicted person crosswise (because it is easier that way) so that they are palm to palm. Also treat the upper back in severe cases.

Reiki treatment with 2nd degree: Mental treatment with suggestions. In severe cases, also use Reiki for the *inner child.*

Natural-healing supplement: Several times daily drink tea made of equal parts of anise and fennel. It should be lukewarm and have a bit of honey in it. Cook an oatmeal soup with water. Be careful: do not cook for more than five minutes. Allow to cool and add some raw milk and honey when it is lukewarm. Eat small portions of it several times daily. Take a tablespoon of fresh onion juice with honey five to ten times a day. Rub the chest with Japanese healing oil or tiger balm.

Visit to a doctor/healing practitioner: If the cough doesn't go away within a week, if it is very severe or blood is coughed up, for example, then a doctor must be consulted.

Visit to a psychotherapist: In general, this is not appropriate.

Cough

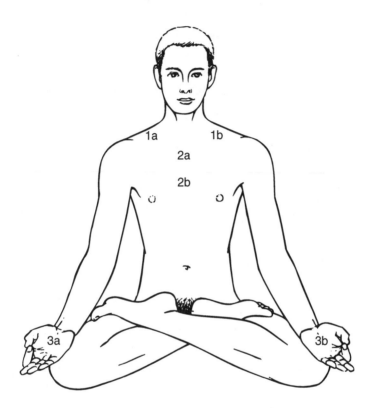

Treatment positions:

1a,b) Collar-bones; 2a,b) middle of chest; 3a,b) palm of hand.

Detoxification/Rejuvenation

General: For thousands of years people from practically every culture have periodically practiced regular detoxification cures to stay healthy or to become so. Probably the best-known and oldest method for this purpose is fasting. The ayurvedic rejuvenation cures and the like are also popular. Detoxification measures can make it easier to heal many types of illness. They give both the psyche and the body more clarity and flexibility. The best time of year to do a cure is in the spring. However, there is no reason not to do such a cure at other times as well.

Reiki treatment with 1st degree: Give the following positions every day for at least four minutes each—1a,b) from the forehead to the teeth, parallel to the nose; 2a,b) on the collarbones; 3) solar plexus; 4) liver/gallbladder—on the right side of the body put one hand on the ribs, ending at the middle of the body, and the other hand directly next to it below; 6a,b) pelvic V, lay the hands together to form a V, from the pelvic bones to the pubic bone; 7a,b) between shoulder and shoulder blades; 8a,b) kidneys; 9a,b) soles of the feet from the toes to the middle of the foot.

Reiki treatment with 2nd degree: Mental healing with affirmations.

Natural-healing supplement: For about four weeks (length of the cure), eliminate from your diet: meat, alcohol, coffee, black tea, refined sugar, table salt and chocolate. Drink at least 1.5 to 2 quarts of water a day. Select a time with little stress for the cure. Three times a day, drink the Swedish Bitters™*, kombucha and wheat-grass juice** (2-3 tbsp.). Add one to two finely-minced garlic cloves to the meals. Once a day, drink a large glass of fresh white-cabbage juice with honey, the juice of half a lemon, some ground caraway, a pinch of fresh dill

---

*Do not use during pregnancy because of its camphor content.
**Or any other drink containing chlorophyll, such as "Kyo-Green" (see suppliers on page 153).

Detoxification/Rejuvenation

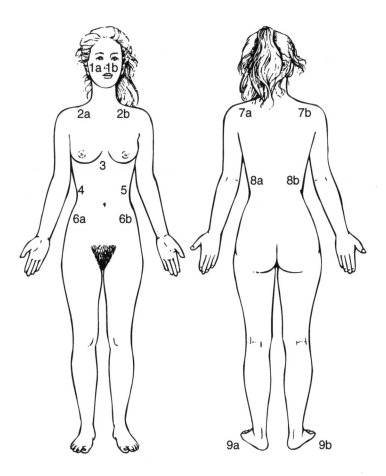

Treatment positions:

1 a,b) Forehead and teeth; 2a,b) collar-bones; 3) solar plexus; 4) liver/gallbladder; 5) spleen/pancreas; 6a,b) pelvic V; 7a,b) between the shoulder and shoulder blades; 8a,b) kidneys; 9a,b) soles of the feet, toes to the middle of the foot.

and a heaping teaspoon of wheat-germ oil. When making the juice, don't use any metal cookware or a steam-juicer. Always drink when very fresh! Stop eating three hours before going to bed. Eat a grated apple (with skin and seeds) with lemon juice, honey, some oat flakes and a spoon of wheat-germ oil every morning. Eat pumpkin and snack on pumpkin seeds regularly. Have a massage once a week and take a sauna twice weekly. Get a lot of easy exercise and take time to listen-inside-yourself. Pray, write poems and paint.

Special case—radioactive detoxification (in case a second Chernobyl occurs): Eat plenty of unpasteurized miso in every form and as much fresh lettuce as possible. Over a longer period of time, drink about half a quart of stinging-nettle juice in several portions. Except for miso, these recommendations come from the nutrition-researcher E. Waerland, whose teachings would also be very beneficial for you.

Visit to the doctor/healing practitioner: Just for safety's sake, it is good to make such a visit before any major detoxification/waste-removal measures. Do this in order to be sure that the body can take the extra exertion created by the elimination of waste matter. The liver, heart and kidneys, as well as the lymph system, need to be examined as to their tolerance for additional strain. If any of these are not fully functional, the cure should be delayed until health has been restored. The doctor should have experience with detoxification/waste-removal cures.

Visit to a psychotherapist: Unnecessary, except when repressed elements and psychological problems arise as a result of detoxification to such a degree that the guidance of a specialist becomes necessary.

Diabetes Mellitus

General: Diabetes mellitus basically appears in two forms: early-onset diabetes (practically incurable) and adult-onset diabetes which can, through a variety of measures, at least be improved and often healed as well. In the case of adult-onset diabetes, there are many factors which play a role such as: overweight, long-term physical or psychological pressure (stress conditioning), heredity and nutritional errors, as well as general damage to the pancreas through toxic overload, for example, as a result of alcohol abuse or consumption of chemically tainted foods. Very frequently the behavior of the afflicted people shows that they can neither properly open up nor set boundaries in parts of their life. This psychological predisposition frequently becomes easily "hereditary" within a family.

Reiki treatment with 1st degree: The following positions should be given on a regular basis, preferably every day and on an empty stomach for at least ten minutes each—1a,b) the tips of the elbows; 2) pancreas (on the left side of body, put one hand on the ribs and reach to the middle of the body with that hand. The other should be exactly beneath it); 3a,b) at the shoulder to the most prominent cervical vertebra toward the front; 4) sacrum; 5a,b) soles of the feet from the toes to at least the middle of the foot.

Reiki treatment with 2nd degree: Mental treatment with suggestions and Reiki for the *inner child* for a lengthier period of time on a regular basis. This is one of the things which is decisive for fundamentally working through the constitutional problems on all levels. In the course of time, the suggestion can change since the disharmony is generally too complex to be covered by one single suggestion. In the case of early-onset diabetes, absolutely do Reiki for the *higher self* as well in order to clarify the path in life.

Natural-healing supplement: The vegetable topinambour can promote the reduction of the blood-sugar level. You can

Diabetes Mellitus

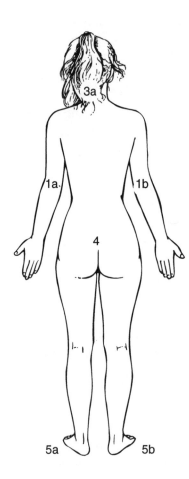

Treatment Positions:

1a,b) The tips of the elbows; 2) pancreas; 3a) nape of the neck, 3b) throat; 4) sacrum; 5a,b) soles of the feet from the toes to at least the middle of the foot.

grow it yourself or get it from a greengrocer. It is delicious raw, as juice and is excellent when cooked, as well as being useful in many ways: for example, as a potato substitute. When eating it raw, let it soak for at least six hours before consuming. Diabetics can eat approximately twice as much topinambour as potatoes. The daily intake of wheat-germ oil and nutritional yeast are to be recommended because the vitamins they contain play a large role in sugar metabolism and facilitate the insulin's work. Otherwise, drink fresh white-cabbage juice (for preparation look under "Detoxification") and eat raw sauerkraut every day. Also use the kombucha. Bean-pod tea can strongly support the lowering of the blood-sugar level (be careful that a sugar deficiency doesn't occur!). The homeopathic remedy Szygium jambolanum 1x can also be useful. Regular exercise often works wonders. If possible, engage in exercise, but avoid high-performance sports. Be careful! Don't do any of this on your own—always inform the attending physician!

Visit to a doctor/healing practitioner: Medical treatment and check-ups on a regular basis must definitely take place. Supplemental actions taken on your own must always be discussed with the doctor or healing practitioner handling the case. By the way, very few general practitioners are actually able to provide specialized treatment for a diabetic. It is therefore worthwhile to visit a special clinic or specialist. A naturopath should do parallel treatment in order to achieve optimum results.

Visit to a psychotherapist: This is at least to be advised in the case of adult-onset diabetes since the resolving of psychological problems, which are often quite concealed, can do much good within the scope of the overall healing process.

Diarrhea

General: Diarrhea is caused by bacteria or parasitic infections and every sort of poisoning, as well as psychological problems. Some medications can cause diarrhea, and it can also be an accompanying symptom of other types of illness. Clarify the cause! Diarrhea is a sign that the body wants to cleanse itself. It should never be simply "stopped." The body must always be helped in its detoxification process so that nothing gets clogged up within it which can lead to secondary diseases and problems with the metabolism.

Reiki treatment with 1st degree: Give the following positions several times a day for at least ten minutes each on a regular basis, until the diarrhea has gone away—1) solar plexus; 2) liver (on the right side of the body, lay one hand starting at the ribs going to the middle of the body, the other one directly beneath it); 3) spleen/pancreas (on the left side of the body, lay one hand starting at the ribs going to the middle of the body); 4a,b) lay one hand on the navel and the other beneath it on the middle of the body.

Reiki treatment with 2nd degree: Mental treatment with suggestions. In severe cases, do Reiki for the *inner child*.

Natural-healing supplement: Use plenty of liquids and salt to replace the loss. If nothing else is available, "cola and salt sticks" is still an old tried and true home remedy. Otherwise, take charcoal pills, healing earth or an apple cure. For this, for up to three days you eat nothing but finely grated apples (with the seeds and skin!), between six to twelve a day. And nothing else! Drink water with a little salt or black, camomile or peppermint tea. But only drink these about an hour before eating or one hour afterwards. Also look under "Fever." Stay away from milk, milk products, meat and everything that is difficult to digest for a period of time even after the disorder has been cured.

Visit to a doctor/healing practitioner: When the diarrhea

Diarrhea

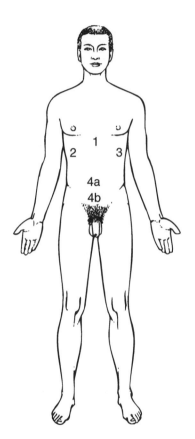

Treatment positions:

1) Solar plexus; 2) liver; 3) spleen/pancreas; 4a) navel, 4b) lower abdomen, mid-body line.

continues over a longer period of time and when blood (black or red) or bits of mucous membrane are in the stool, go immediately to the doctor. Specialized intervention is necessary due to the threat of too much fluid loss, and the causes must be clarified in this situation.

Visit to a psychotherapist: This is only recommended when there is a frequent recurrence or in the case of an illness without a clear physical cause (psychosomatic diarrhea).

Fear/Dread

General: Fear and dread should be advisers, but not rulers. Every healthy person is capable of experiencing them. They only become abnormal when we are ruled by them and suffer as a result, or when they are declared to be non-existent and the feelings connected with them are not conscious.

Reiki treatment with 1st degree: In the case of acute fear, give the following positions at least fifteen minutes each— 2) solar plexus; 3a,b) pelvic V, lay the hands together to form a V from the pelvic bones to the pubic bone. To bring about a change the mental attitude over the long term, give the following positions 1) to 6) for at least four minutes each and 7) for at least six minutes—1a,b) lay the hands parallel to the nose from the forehead to the teeth; 2) solar plexus; 3a,b) pelvic V; 4a,b) shoulder blades; 5a,b) kidneys; 6a) sacrum, 6b) coccyx (this hand must lay beneath the coccyx to the perineum); 7a,b) soles of the feet from the toes to at least the middle of the foot.

Reiki treatment with 2nd degree: Mental healing with affirmations.

Natural-healing supplement: For a longer period of time, drink several glasses of kombucha before meals. The first glass in the morning should be with a good teaspoon of naturally pure honey from ecological cultivation. If this doesn't appeal to you, then take the honey in warm water alone. Add wheatgrass juice* (2-3 tbsp.) to soups and sauces when they have cooled off a bit. Drink valerian-root tea regularly: mornings soak two teaspoons in a half a pint of cold water and let brew until the evening, then strain. Warm slightly, sweeten with a bit of honey and drink before going to sleep.

Visit to a doctor/healing practitioner: Classic homeopathy and Bach flower essences can work true wonders here.

Visit to a psychotherapist: Definitely do psychotherapy in difficult and stubborn cases!

---

*Or any other drink containing chlorophyll, such as "Kyo-Green" (see suppliers on page 153).

Fear/Dread

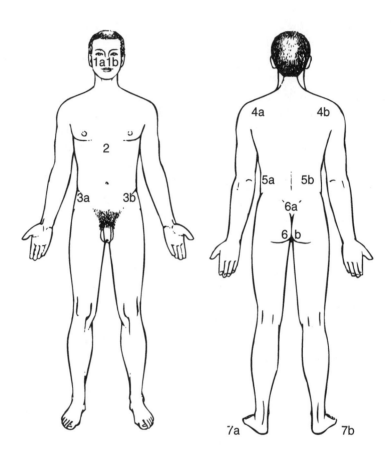

Treatment positions:

1a,b) The hands parallel to the nose from the forehead to the teeth; 2) solar plexus; 3a,b) pelvic V; 4a,b) shoulder blades; 5a,b) kidneys; 6a) sacrum, 6b) coccyx to the perineum; 7a,b) soles of the feet from the toes to the middle of the foot.

Fever

General: Fever is an appropriate reaction by the body for fighting an infection. Fever should not be interfered with as long as it doesn't exceed the tolerance of the afflicted person or get higher than about 104° degrees Fahrenheit. The fever should not be reduced too quickly since heart/circulatory problems may occur as a result. You should therefore always wait for the reaction to an application and do not do anything too quickly, except in the case of emergencies.

Reiki treatment with 1st degree: 1a,b) From the forehead to the teeth, parallel to the nose; 2a,b) ears; 3) back of the head; 4) solar plexus; 5a,b) liver and gallbladder—on the right side of the body, the upper hand aligned with the ribs and reaching to the middle of the body, the other directly beneath it;6a,b) sacrum and from beneath the coccyx to the perineum; 7a,b) soles of the feet from the toes to at least the middle of the foot.

Reiki treatment with 2nd degree: Mental treatment with suggestions.

Natural-healing supplement: Rub down the soles of the feet with freshly cut onions and then use them to make a foot wrap. Replace it every few hours. Drink ginger or black tea. Do an "alcohol rub," rubbing down the entire body with high-proof alcohol. Don't use liqueurs since they are too sticky! Drink cherry juice or eat raw cherries. Eat pieces of dried apple (not sulphurized!). Drink tea from made of fresh garlic (one pressed clove per quart) or peppercorns (10 roughly crushed corns per quart). Don't drink too much at once and eat a bit of something beforehand. This is not necessarily good for people with sensitive stomachs. When the wrists are bathed in cold water, this cools the entire body.

Visit to a doctor/healing practitioner: Absolutely necessary only in cases of high fever, more than about 102 degrees Fahrenheit, and lasting longer than three days continuously or when there are frequent interludes with recurring fever.

Visit to a psychotherapist: Not appropriate.

Fever

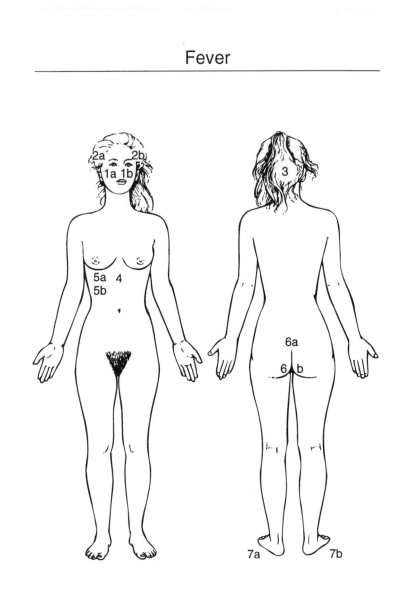

Treatment positions:

1a,b) Forehead to the teeth, parallel to the nose; 2a,b) ears; 3) back of the head; 4) solar plexus; 5a,b) liver and gallbladder; 6a,b) sacrum and from beneath the coccyx to the perineum; 7a,b) soles of the feet, toes to the foot middle.

Flu

General: In cases where the flu occurs frequently within short intervals, a weakness of the immune system can exist. The true viral influenza is a dangerous infection that absolutely must be treated by a doctor. Also look under "Fever."

Reiki treatment with 1st degree: Give the following positions daily for at least five minutes each until the illness has been cured—1a,b) Soles of the feet from the tips of the toes to at least the middle of the foot; 2a,b) grasp the wrists; 3a,b) cross the hands of the client (because it's easier) and hold them so that they are palm to palm; 4) solar plexus; 5a,b) thymus gland directly beneath the throat and the heart beneath it; 6a,b) pelvic V, lay the hands forming a V from the pelvic bones to the pubic bone.

Reiki treatment with 2nd degree: Mental treatment with suggestions. In the case of true viral influenza (see above), it is essential to give Reiki for the *inner child* and the *higher self.*

Natural-healing supplement: Take up to ten tablespoons of carrot syrup made in the following manner every day: Boil carrot juice with brown sugar to make a thick syrup. Store in a sealed container. Onion compress: Coarsely grate or cut raw onions and make a throat wrap, which should be changed hourly. Alternately drink elder or linden-flower tea to "sweat out" the illness. Keep warm and avoid drafts. Eat two finely grated apples (with seeds and skin) and raw carrots with honey and lemon juice every day.

Visit to a doctor/healing practitioner: In cases of periodically recurring illness, a treatment by a qualified naturopath is highly recommended. If you are ill with a form of viral influenza, consult a doctor immediately!

Visit to a psychotherapist: Not appropriate.

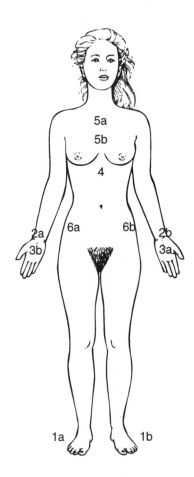

Treatment positions:

1a,b) Soles of the feet, toe tips to foot middle; 2a,b) wrists; 3a,b) palms; 4) solar plexus; 5a,b) thymus gland and heart; 6a,b) pelvic V.

Hair Loss

General: Hair loss can be a side effect from medication, metabolic diseases, infections, excessive psychological strain, long-term malnutrition, as an accompanying symptom of other types of illness or through hereditary disposition (the latter mainly for men). Hereditary disposition to hair loss can be effectively delayed, but according to all the reliable information I have at hand, it cannot really be healed. In other cases, assuming the roots of the hair haven't died, there is quite a bit that treatment with natural remedies can do. However, patience and staying power are important in every case.

Reiki treatment with 1st degree: Supply the following positions with Reiki for at least five minutes each every day—1a,b) from the forehead to the teeth, parallel to the nose; 2) head area where there is hair loss; 3) solar plexus; 4a,b) pelvic V, lay the hands in a V shape from the pelvic bones to the pubic bone; 5a,b) kidneys; 6a) sacrum, 6b) from beneath the pubic bone to the perineum. As often as possible between the treatments, treat 2) as a supporting measure.

Reiki treatment with 2nd degree: Mental treatment with suggestions. In severe cases, give Reiki for the *inner child.*

Natural-healing supplement: Switch to high-quality vegetarian food. Pay extra attention to getting enough vitamin A, B-complex, C and E as well as minerals and trace elements and organic high-quality protein. Since vitamin A and E as well as certain minerals can cause problems when given in an overdose, work with a doctor of natural healing when taking them on a long-term basis. Drink at least two glasses of kombucha and take wheat-grass juice* (2-3 tbsp. juice 3 times a day) and a tablespoon of honey every day. Massage the head thoroughly after washing the hair, alternating a little bit of wheat-germ oil or stinging-nettle tea regularly. Massage the

---

*Or any other drink containing chlorophyll, such as "Kyo-Green" (see suppliers on page 153).

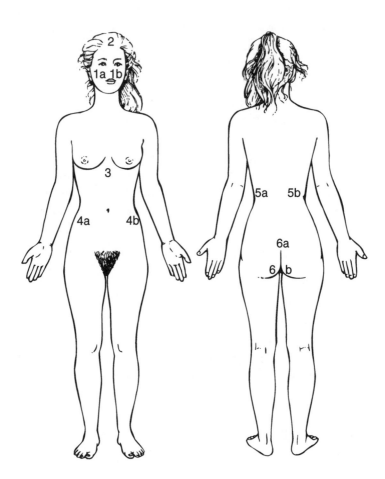

Treatment positions:

1a,b) Forehead to teeth, parallel to the nose; 2) head area where there is hair loss; 3) solar plexus; 4a,b) pelvic V; 5a,b) kidneys; 6a) sacrum, 6b) from beneath the pubic bone to the perineum.

scalp well two to three times a week with a sliced onion half. If the hair loss has a psychological cause: take two tablets of Calcium Phosphoricum 6x three times daily, ten drops of – Rescue Remedy made from Bach flower essences twice daily over a longer period. After washing the hair, rinse it with a glass of water which has had five drops of Rescue Remedy from a stock bottle mixed into it.

Visit to a doctor/healing practitioner: To be on the safe side, this should always be done in order to determine in time whether other types of illness may possibly be the originating factors. In many cases there are a myriad of well-tried possibilities which the naturopath has available to stop hair loss.

Visit to a psychotherapist: This is only useful when organic and hereditary factors can be eliminated and the usual healing methods don't bring results.

Headache

General: Headaches can be a *symptom* for a variety of disorders: an excess of physical or emotional strain, weather influences, climatic changes, sleep deprivation, misuse of stimulants, extreme emotional outbursts, stress, head injuries, displacement of the cervical spine, subacute or chronic inflammations in the head and throat area, as well as chemical or nutritional poisoning. Also see "Migraine" and "Detoxification."

Reiki treatment with 1st degree: Try out the following positions and continue to use only the effective ones until the person's symptoms disappear. Headaches can have very different causes and are treated in different way because of this. Give the effective positions several times a day for at least ten minutes each—1a,b) temples or wherever it hurts; 2a,b) soles of the feet from the tips of the toes to the foot middle (energetic blockage in the head area); 3a,b) nape of neck and shoulders (muscle tension); 4) sacrum, and then 5a,b) pelvic V, lay the hands together to form a V from the pelvic bones to the pubic bone (disharmony in the pelvic area, first and second chakra); 6a) solar plexus, 6b) liver (upset stomach/indigestion). When the headache is one-sided and doesn't respond to the other positions: 7a) the wrist on the same side and 7b) treat the middle of the underarm with each hand, then 8a) lay the hands palm to palm and with the other hand 8b) treat the upper arm at the shoulderjoint.

Reiki treatment with 2nd degree: Mental treatment with suggestions. In severe cases and for long-term harmonizing, use Reiki for the *inner child.*

Natural-healing supplement: Drink the kombucha three to four times a day. Take footbaths with strong, hot ginger-root tea until the headaches have let up for the most part or have completely disappeared. Put quark (curd cheese) that is not too cold in a dish towel and lay it on the forehead and temples.

Headache

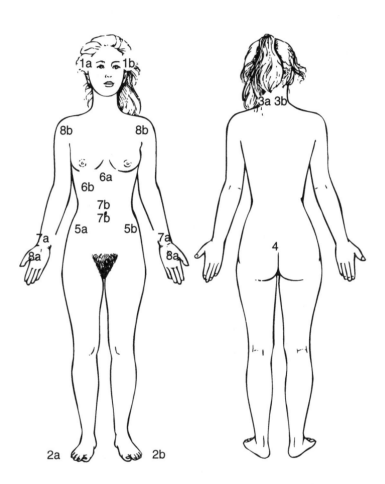

Treatment positions:

1a,b) Temples (or wherever it hurts); 2a,b) foot soles, toe tips to foot middle; 3a,b) nape of neck and shoulders; 4) sacrum; 5a,b) pelvic V; 6a) solar plexus, 6b) liver; 7a) wrist, 7b) middle of the underarm; 8a) palms, 8b) upper arm at the shoulder joint.

Visit to a doctor/healing practitioner: If headaches keep appearing or last for a longer period of time, definitely consult a healing practitioner, neurologist, spine specialist or a Feldenkrais therapist, in order to get an exact diagnosis and to initiate therapeutic measures.

Visit to a psychotherapist: If no organic causes are found and the normal healing methods are not successful, it is a good idea to seek psychotherapeutic treatment.

Hemorrhoids

General: Some of the causes of hemorrhoids are: a lifestyle with a great deal of sitting, not enough physical exercise, faulty nutrition, frequent constipation and hormonal influences in connection with menstruation or pregnancy. Other causes can be hereditary weakness of certain veins or connective tissue, blockage in the area of the portal vein or liver disorders. General or specific disturbances in the circulation of the bodily fluids or abnormal swelling of the rectal veins can cause hemorrhoids. A disharmony of the psyche is also among the fundamental causes.

Reiki treatment with 1st degree: Treat the following positions over a longer period time daily for at least six minutes each—1a,b) sacrum, one hand directly above the fold of the buttock, the other above the first; 2a) sacrum, above the fold of the buttock, 2b) from beneath the coccyx to the perineum; 3a,b) on the back at the waist, don't treat the spine directly; 4) solar plexus; 5a,b) soles of the feet from the tips of the toes to the foot middle. In addition, do particularly 4) more frequently and also supply the entire stomach area with Reiki.

Reiki treatment with 2nd degree: Mental healing with affirmations. In severe cases, also Reiki for the inner child.

Natural-healing supplement: When nothing else is available, two home remedies can effectively help hemorrhoids that have become inflamed: peel a not too small garlic clove and with a very sharp knife make a few small surface cuts in it; use as a suppository. Or cut fresh ginger root into a suppository form and use it as such. Both methods are only meant as emergency measures, since longer usage can lead to skin irritation. In general, this will occur more quickly with garlic than with ginger. For long-term use, witch-hazel or calendula ointment or honey are well suited. Be sure there is a regular bowel movement; also look under "Constipation" for this purpose. At the least, strongly limit alcohol, smoking coffee and hot spices.

Hemorrhoids

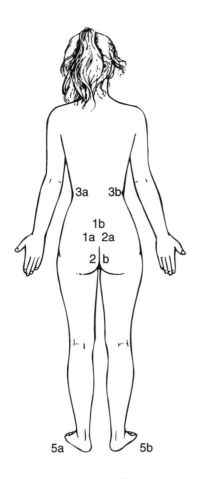

Treatment positions:

1a,b) Sacrum, one hand above the fold of the buttocks, the other above the first; 2a) sacrum, above the fold of the buttocks, 2b) from beneath the coccyx to the perineum; 3a,b) the back, right and left of the spine at waist level; 4) solar plexus; 5a,b) soles of the feet, tips of the toes to the middle of the foot.

Until a lasting cure has been achieved, it would be best to entirely eliminate them. Vegetarian, high-quality nutrition with dietary fiber is very useful. Regular exercise helps, but not high-performance sport. Eat at least one tomato with every meal and at least one finely minced raw garlic clove daily. Drink two to three glasses of kombucha.

Homeopathic: Once a day, take one tablet of Calcium Fluoratum 12x and, over a longer period, twice daily two tablets of Silicea 6x for strengthening the connective tissue and vessels. Also let one tablet of Magnesium Phosphoricum 12x dissolve in the mount about fifteen minutes before eating to harmonize the balance of the psyche.

Visit to a doctor/healing practitioner: Should take place just to be sure there are no other serious disorders in the intestinal area. Operative removal is seldom necessary and is purely symptomatic. An experienced naturopath can and should find deeper causes, as well as helping to heal difficult cases.

Visit to a psychotherapist: This is only appropriate in stubborn cases as a supportive measure.

Hoarseness

General: Hoarseness can have relatively harmless causes like: over-exertion of the vocal apparatus, misuse of nicotine and alcohol, colds and flu infections, chronic bronchitis or tension in the throat area; however, it can also be, particularly in chronic cases, a symptom of a more serious illness.

Reiki treatment with 1st degree: Give the following positions several times daily for at least ten minutes each until the illness is cured—1a,b) Front of the throat, without the hands making contact; 2a,b) collar-bones; 3) solar plexus.

Reiki treatment with 2nd degree: In the case of frequent attacks and chronic illness, mental treatment with suggestions.

Natural-healing supplement: Take fresh onion juice mixed with honey several times daily. Gargle with an apple-cider vinegar/honey-water mixture or with ginger tea. Reflect upon whether or not what you say really reflects what you mean. Or does it frighten you, are you insecure about it, are you tensing up as a result or lying to yourself about it?

Visit to a doctor/healing practitioner: In severe and chronic cases, definitely go to a doctor in order to get an exact diagnosis and early detection as well as treatment of any existing type of serious illness.

Visit to a psychotherapist: Only appropriate when no organic causes can be found and the usual healing methods aren't successful.

Hoarseness

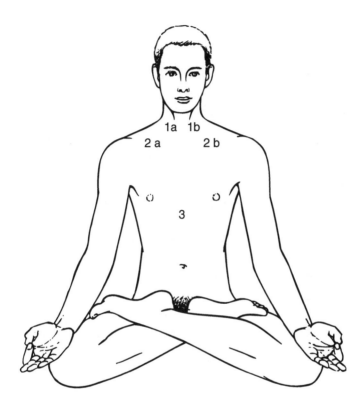

Treatment positions:

Give the following positions several times a day for at least ten minutes each until cured—1a,b) front side of the throat, without the hands making contact; 2a,b) collar-bones; 3) solar plexus.

Immune-System Deficiencies (not AIDS!)

General: A great many people have immune systems which are intermittently or even chronically weakened. This shows itself especially in the tendency toward colds and infections, as well as general weariness and lack of energy.

Reiki treatment with 1st degree: Give the following positions over a longer period of time daily for five minutes each— 1a,b) from the forehead to the teeth, parallel to the nose; 2a,b) collar-bones; 3a) solar plexus, 3b) liver; 4a,b) pelvic V, lay the hands together to form a V from the pelvic bones to the pubic bone; 5a,b) on the back side of the body, beneath the throat from the prominent cervical vertebrae to the front; 6a) sacrum, 6b) from beneath the coccyx to the perineum.

Reiki treatment with 2nd degree: Mental healing with affirmations and Reiki for the *inner child*.

Natural-healing supplement: Switch to a vegetarian diet. Eliminate alcohol, refined sugar, chocolate, white flour and coffee from diet. Take an echinacea preparation for a longer period of time. Drink three glasses of kombucha and the wheatgrass juice* (2-3 tbsp. of juice 3 times a day) and honey, as well as one or two finely-minced raw garlic cloves divided in portions at mealtimes. On a regular basis, eat raw, unpasteurized sauerkraut or fresh white-cabbage salad with red paprika and onions in small portions distributed throughout the day.

Visit to a doctor/healing practitioner: A naturopath is essential in stubborn cases!

Visit to a psychotherapist: Only useful when no organic causes are found and the usual healing methods show little effect.

---

*Or any other drink containing chlorophyll, such as "Kyo-Green" (see suppliers on page 153).

Immune-System Deficiencies (not AIDS!)

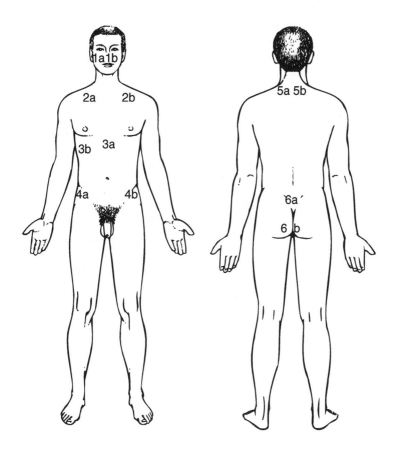

Treatment positions:

1a,b) Forehead to the teeth, parallel to the nose; 2a,b) collarbones; 3a) solar plexus, 3b) liver; 4a,b) pelvic V; 5a,b) beneath the throat from the prominent cervical vertebrae to the front; 6a) sacrum, 6b) from beneath the coccyx to the perineum.

Insect Bites

General: For people who are allergic to the particular poison, an insect bite can have life-threatening consequences. Some people get stung more frequently than others. This is surely no accident ... Look at an acupuncture chart to see which meridians or points the stings are on and find out about their meaning. You will often suddenly see the light as a result. Acupuncture points in need of treatment are energetically weaker than their healthy surroundings. The insects sense these places which have an energetically "lowered resistance" with their sensitive feelers and fly to these less protected areas of the skin to land.

Reiki treatment with 1st degree: Immediately treat the sting point directly without skin contact. To lessen the tendency to be stung in the long term, use positions 1) and 3) daily at least five minutes each for a longer time, applying the third for at least ten minutes—1a,b) from the forehead to the teeth, parallel to the nose; 2a,b) pelvic V, lay the hands together to form a V from the pelvic bones to the pubic bone; 3) solar plexus.

Reiki treatment with 2nd degree: For frequently occurring insect bites, do mental treatment with suggestions.

Natural-healing supplement: If it can be seen, remove the stinger immediately with the fingernails and suck out the wound. Then lay slices of onion or lemon on it or rub fresh garlic or slightly moistened salt into it. This also works with olive oil, toothpaste or moist healing earth.

Visit to a doctor/healing practitioner: In the case of allergic reactions, breathing difficulty, hornet's stings or stings close to nerve centers, larger blood vessels or in the respiratory system and ears, immediately go to the doctor!

Visit to a psychotherapist: Not appropriate.

Insect Bites

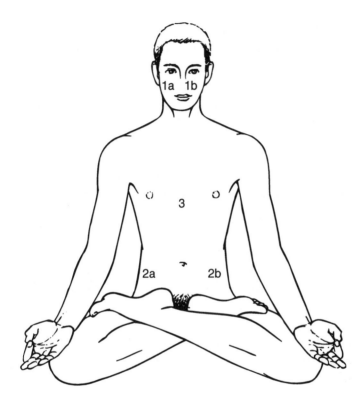

Treatment positions:

1a,b) Forehead to the teeth, parallel to the nose; 2a,b) pelvic V; 3) solar plexus.

Lumbago

General: Through awkward movement, unaccustomed physical work, overexertion, lifting of heavier loads, becoming drenched and chilled, lumbago can suddenly occur. Lumbago frequently appears among the elderly through symptoms of exhaustion and attrition. The pain mainly radiates outwards from the spine. It comes on suddenly and dramatically.

Reiki treatment with 1st degree: Treat the following positions regularly, several times a day, at least ten minutes each—1a) sacrum, 1b) prominent cervical vertebrae directly under the shoulder. In addition, 2a,b) the area to the right and left of the spine, in which the pain center lies, and 3a,b) the inner side of the feet from the big toe to the heels.

Reiki treatment with 2nd degree: mental treatment with suggestions and Reiki for the *inner child* over a longer period of time.

Natural-healing supplement: Drink chamomile tea and do warm compresses with strong chamomile tea. Drink warm (not hot!) elderberry juice and a half glass of water three to five times daily. Rub in Japanese healing oil or tiger balm. Put on several layers of white-cabbage leaves (application is described under "Sore Throat"') and keep warm. Change about every two hours. Rub in stinging-nettle spirits. Learn to do Feldenkrais exercises.

Visit with a doctor/healing practitioner: An experienced naturopath should definitely be consulted in order to have an exact diagnosis done and eliminate the possibility of any type of concealed, severe illness, as well as initiating effective therapy measures in stubborn cases.

Visit to a psychotherapist: In general, this is not appropriate.

Lumbago

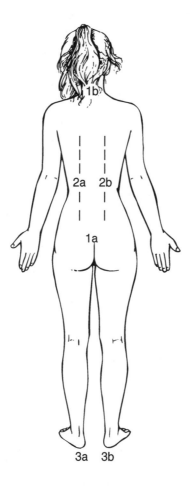

Treatment positions:

1a) Sacrum, 1b) prominent cervical vertebrae directly beneath the shoulder; 2a,b) the area to the right and left of the spine, in which the pain center lies; 3a,b) the inner side of the foot from the big toe to the heels.

Mental Disability

General: Mental disabilities can be congenital or develop as a result of an accident or illness. It is *always* worth not seeing the condition as unchangeable, but rather to try to at least improve it. Comprehensive studies have repeatedly shown that improvement, perhaps even to an extensive degree, is possible through loving care and the appropriate methods, even in severe cases. The various manifestations of mental disabilities are naturally so complex that I can't handle this topic to a full extent within this context. For further study, I suggest you see the literature in the annotated bibliography.

Reiki treatment with 1st degree: At least twice a week on a regular basis for a longer period of time, give the following positions for at least fifteen minutes each—1a,b) the inner side of the feet, the same reflex zone as used by the metamorphic method (see book suggestions in Index l). If your hand isn't large enough to cover the whole reflex zone at one time, first treat the front area and then work toward the heels. Before every Reiki session, give a circular massage with a very light touch to the area to be treated for about five minutes. The following positions are extra but supplementary when given for at least five minutes each on a regular basis—2a,b) from the forehead to the teeth, parallel to the nose; 3a,b) ears; 4a) solar plexus, 4b) heart chakra; 5a,b) cross the client's hands (because its more comfortable) and take them so that they are palm to palm. In conclusion, treat the soles of the feet from the toes to the middle of the foot for at least three minutes.

Reiki treatment with 2nd degree: Mental healing with chosen suggestions. If the affected person is not in a position to ask a question and select a suggestion themselves, the person closest to them should do it for them. He or she should do this by concentrating on the affected person for awhile, becoming inwardly empty themselves and attempting to act on the person's behalf. Furthermore, the *inner child* as well as the *higher self* should receive Reiki regularly.

106

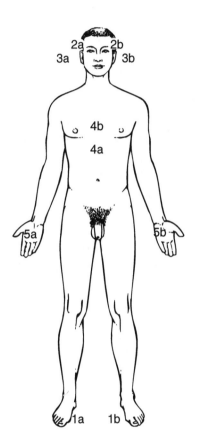

Treatment positions:

1a,b) The inner side of the feet; 2a,b) from the forehead to the teeth, parallel to the nose; 3a,b) ears; 4a) solar plexus, 4a) heart chakra; 5a,b) the hands crossed, palm to palm.

Natural-healing supplement: The long-term use of the metamorphic method can be highly recommended. This is a special massage system which practically everyone, even a small child, can easily learn and apply successfully. I refer you to the book recommendations in the annotated bibliography and courses on the topic which are sometimes even offered at adult evening schools. However, the metamorphic method can also easily be learned from the book. Aside from this, over a longer period of time give one garlic clove evenly distributed among the meals every day. Always use garlic which is fresh and do not heat it very much. Phosphates should be eliminated from the diet. Nutritional counseling at a consumer agency will inform you as to which foods contain them.

Visit to a doctor/healing practitioner: Classic homeopathy, acupuncture or acupressure and Bach flower essences frequently accomplish things that are almost unbelievable, even in severe cases. The appropriate specialists should be consulted for this purpose. However, the treatment will always take some time. It's always worth it to be patient!

Visit to a psychotherapist: Can be very important for the mentally disabled person, but is usually not continually necessary in most cases. However, the person closest to them should participate in a series of therapy sessions in order to better deal with the long-term caretaking without getting too intensively stuck in his or her own problems and fears.

Migraine

General: Sensitive, mentally flexible and achievement-oriented people who are objectively or subjectively under continued stress, and don't have the ability to take free time and allow themselves to relax, often get migraines. These can be brought on by changes in the weather, hot winds and the like, although these are not the causes. Most of the time there is a hereditary disposition toward them.

Reiki treatment with 1st degree: Give the following positions several times daily for at least six minutes each and repeat over a longer period of time. The treatment should start immediately when the first signs of a migraine occur: 1) solar plexus; 2a,b) temples; 3a,b) from the temples above the ears, lay the hands in a diagonally upward direction; 4a,b) pelvic V, lay the hands to form a V from the pelvic bones to the pubic bone; 5a,b) soles of the feet from the tips of the toes to at least the middle of the foot. Also frequently massage both ear lobs until they are well-supplied with blood, and then hold them for a few minutes with the thumb, index and middle finger. Massage the inner side of the big toe, across from the next toe, and then cover with as many fingers as fit on it and hold for a few minutes. To decrease the disposition toward migraines, give positions 1), 4a,b) and 5a,b) for at least ten minutes each for a longer period of time every day.

Reiki treatment with 2nd degree: Mental treatment with suggestions; for a long-term change to a harmonious lifestyle, use Reiki for the *inner child* and the *higher self.*

Natural-healing supplement: Grate a piece of horseradish root the length of an index finger and briefly let it boil in 1 quart of red wine. Then let simmer for an hour with a low flame and a covered pot. Take one to two teaspoons from this drink once an hour until the migraine subsides.

Attention: In cases of kidney illness, don't take horseradish wine until consulting the attending doctor about it. Multiple-

Migraine

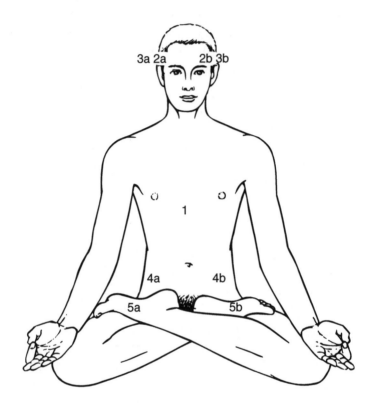

Treatment positions:

1) Solar plexus; 2a,b) temples; 3a,b) from the temples above the ears in a diagonally upward direction; 4a,b) pelvic V; 5a,b) soles of the feet, toe tips to the foot middle.

layered white-cabbage compresses (for application, see "Sore Throat") should be put on the forehead and temples. Drink melissa tea with honey on a regular basis (also during times without symptoms). Rub the temples, the forehead and the stomach area with several drops of best-quality lavender oil. Put a lavender sachet under your pillow. Learn to permit yourself to relax and "turn off."

Visit to a doctor/healing practitioner: In the case of frequently occurring migraines, an experienced natural healer should be consulted so that an exact diagnosis can be made and appropriate therapeutic measures can be initiated, when required.

Visit to a psychotherapist: A psychotherapist can be useful when no organic causes can be found and the usual healing methods don't bring satisfying results.

Neck Tenseness
(Shoulder-Hand-Syndrome)

General: There are many causes for this troublesome disorder, which often strongly reduces the quality of life. Some of the possible causes are: inflammatory processes in the shoulder-hand area, rheumatic, delayed damage from injuries or calcium deposits as a result of decreased use of these joints.

Reiki treatment with 1st degree: Give the following positions for a longer time at least six minutes each every day— 1a,b) throat on the back; 2a,b) from prominent cervical vertebrae beneath the shoulder to the front; 3) solar plexus; 4a,b) take the crossed hands (because it is more comfortable) so that they are palm to palm; 5a,b) upper arm at the shoulder-joint.

Reiki treatment with 2nd degree: Mental treatment with suggestions. In difficult cases, also use Reiki for the *inner child.*
Natural-healing supplement: Switch to a vegetarian, high-quality diet. Eliminate alcohol and salt for a longer period of time. While you have the symptoms and even after the complaints are gone, exercise with special remedial gymnastics, Qi Gong, Feldenkrais or Tai Chi Chuan with *competent guidance* for a longer period time. Drink several glasses of kombucha every day. Be sure to get increased quantities of vitamin C, E and the B-complex. Undertake a basic intestinal cleansing under the direction of a qualified naturopath.

Visit to a doctor/healing practitioner: In difficult and stubborn cases, a careful examination by an experienced naturopath is always important since these symptoms can also show up in connection with other types of severe illness. If required, use the recommended therapy.

Visit to a psychotherapist: Appropriate in stubborn cases.

Neck Tenseness
(Shoulder-Hand-Syndrome)

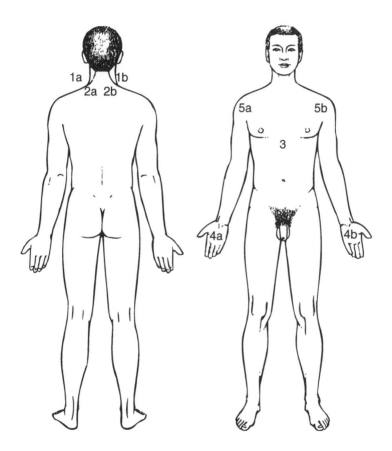

Treatment positions:

1a,b) Throat on the back; 2a,b) from prominent cervical vertebrae beneath the shoulder to the front; 3) solar plexus; 4a,b) palm; 5a,b) upper arm at shoulderjoint.

Nervousness

General: Nervousness is a general phrase for many different disorders of the vegetative system; the physical aspects have a close relationship with the emotional in this respect. The unity of psyche (mind) and soma (body) is disturbed, perhaps because of stress, the feeling of overwork, a disharmonious life style or too much brooding and not enough living. Traumas which have not been worked out can also cause nervousness, which in time can cause psychosomatic diseases.

Reiki treatment with 1st degree: Give the following positions over a longer time every day for at least six minutes each—1a,b) from the forehead to the teeth, parallel to the nose; 2a,b) temples; 3a) solar plexus together with 3b) lower abdomen. Give these last two positions for at least twelve minutes!; 4a,b) soles of the feet from the tips of the toes to the foot middle.

Reiki treatment with 2nd degree: mental treatment with suggestions and Reiki for the *inner child.*

Natural-healing supplement: Melissa tea with honey; green oat tea or oat as a homeopathic remedy: Avena Sativa1x, three to four times daily, ten to twenty drops. Set aside one day a week for raw foods only. Give up coffee, chocolate, cocoa and black tea. Increase your intake of vitamin B-complex, E, C and lecithin. Learn Tai Chi Chuan or yoga.

Visit to a doctor/healing practitioner: If the nervousness continues for a longer period of time or if it represents a stronger impairment in your lifestyle, an experienced naturopath should be consulted.

Visit to a psychotherapist: This should definitely take place in stubborn cases where the usual healing methods don't create a reaction. An examination by a neurologist should also occur.

Nervousness

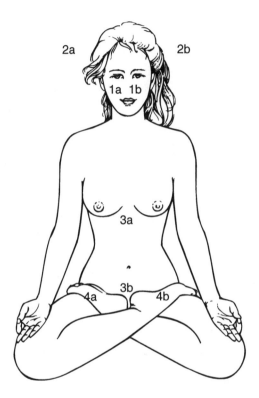

Treatment positions:

1a,b) Forehead to the teeth, parallel to the nose; 2a,b) temples;
3a) solar plexus, 3b) lower abdomen; 4a,b) soles of the feet, toe
tips to foot middle.

Obesity

General: Obesity can usually be traced to false eating habits and psychological causes. In only 3% of the cases is the reason glandular or metabolic disturbances. Anyone who weighs more than ten percent above the normal weight is overweight.

Reiki treatment with 1st degree: Give the following positions over a longer period of time every day for at least four minutes each—1a,b) from the forehead to the teeth, parallel to the nose; 2a,b) temples; 3a,b) front of the throat, but please don't touch with the hands; 4a,b) liver and gallbladder—on the right side of the body—the upper hand lies even with the costal arch reaching toward the middle of the body, the other hand right beneath it; 6a,b) pelvic V, the hands form a V from the pelvic bones to the pubic bone; 7a,b) one hand above and one hand below the navel; 8a,b) soles of the feet, from the tips of the toes to at least the middle of the foot.

Reiki treatment with 2nd degree: Mental healing with affirmations. Give Reiki for the *inner child* in severe cases.

Natural-healing supplement: The Beverly Hills Diet by Judy Mazel (see the annotated bibliography) if the attending physician has no objections. It is absolutely necessary to include some kind of sport that *is fun* in the life structure! In addition, drink the Swedish Bitters™* and much kombucha three times a day. Think about what activities, besides eating, could bring enjoyment and try them out. Engage in hobbies that are simply playful fun. What does the fat protect you from? Which experiences that frighten you are you avoiding from behind the protective wall of your armour of fat? Weight loss has nothing to do with an act of the will, but rather with more harmonious and natural ways to satisfy your needs. Under no circumstances should "appetite suppressors" be taken! Always try to exactly clarify the causes on all levels. As an aside: certain extreme weight ideals are also "fashionable."

---

*Do not use during pregnancy because of its camphor content.

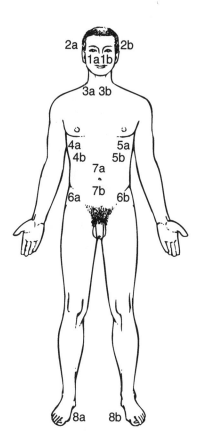

Treatment positions:

1a,b) Forehead to the teeth, parallel to the nose; 2a,b) temples; 3a,b) front of the throat; 4a,b) liver and gallbladder; 5a,b) spleen and pancreas; 6a,b) pelvic V; 7a,b) one hand above and the other below the navel; 8a,b) soles of the feet, tips of the toes to the foot middle.

Visit to a doctor/healing practitioner: Classic homeopathy, Bach flower essences, acupuncture or acupressure, as well as other natural-healing methods can offer very effective help. They should be applied by someone specialized in the particular method who can also determine, for example, if thyroid-gland disorders, diabetes mellitus or other severe forms of illness exist. They can help put together an individually suitable diet as well.

Visit to a psychotherapist: If no organic causes can be determined in cases of considerable, lengthy and continuing overweight or sudden weight gain, definitely make such a visit. NLP, a modern therapy method, can help a great deal. However, it is always necessary to have a genuine personal wish for a different type of lifestyle without overweight.

PMS (Premenstrual Syndrome)

General: The causes are hormonal swings in the female cycle—and a woman's mostly subconscious psychological problem of fully accepting this expression of her sexuality. PMS is usually very stubborn: an indication of how important a reconciliation with her own womanhood is to nature.

Reiki treatment with 1st degree: Give the following positions over a longer time, starting at latest by ovulation to the end of the PMS, at least seven minutes each—1a,b) from the forehead to the teeth, parallel to the nose; 2a) heart, 2b) solar plexus; 3a,b) pelvic V, lay the hands to form a V from the pelvic bones to the pubic bone; 4a) forehead and third eye together with 4b) second chakra on lower abdomen, directly above pubic bone in the middle of the body; 5a,b) take the crossed hands (more comfortable), so that they are palm to palm.

Reiki treatment with 2nd degree: Give mental treatment with suggestions and Reiki for the *inner child.*

Natural-healing supplement: Increase the supply of vitamin B-complex, particularly B6 after ovulation. In addition, take borage oil and melissa tea with honey on a regular basis over a longer period of time. Do moon meditations with a moonstone between the hands and a carnelian on the second chakra. While doing so, look at the moon and simply feel for at least thirty minutes. Meditate on the Tarot card "The High Priestess" and think about the rhythms of the creation, like day and night, life and death and particularly the spiritual meaning of your womanhood and how you can live and enjoy it in daily life.

Visit to a doctor/healing practitioner: A naturopath should be consulted in difficult cases. Holistic medicine offers many possibilities for healing PMS.

Visit to a psychotherapist: This is very helpful in stubborn cases.

PMS (Premenstrual Syndrome)

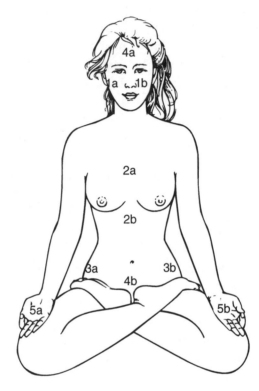

Treatment positions:

1a,b) Forehead to teeth, parallel to the nose; 2a) heart, 2b) solar plexus; 3a,b) pelvic V; 4a) forehead and third eye, 4b) lower abdomen, above the pubic bone; 5a,b) palms.

Pregnancy

General: Naturally pregnancy is not an illness, although it is often treated as such these days. The instructions offered here are meant to help the psyche and body better handle the increased demands and make the experience of the pregnancy happier and more natural.

Reiki treatment with 1st degree: Give the following positions during the entire pregnancy on a daily basis for at least five minutes each—1a,b) temples; 2a) heart, 2b) solar plexus; 3a,b) pelvic V, lay the hands to form a V from the pelvic bones to the pubic bone; 4a) liver, 4b) spleen/pancreas; 5a,b) kidneys; 6a) sacrum first with 6b) connection to thigh on the right outer leg with 6c) like 6b) only the left thigh; 7a,b) soles of the feet from the toe tips to the middle of the foot. In between times, the entire abdominal area as often as possible and treat 5a,b). A few weeks after the birth, give 1a,b); 2b); 3a,b) and 6a).

Reiki treatment with 2nd degree: mental treatment with selected suggestions and Reiki for the *inner child.*

Natural-healing supplement: Be sure to eat foods that are basically easy to digest and pay attention to increased levels of vital materials (vitamins, minerals, trace elements; enzymes and so forth) to accommodate the situation.

Caution! Vitamin A should not be taken in an isolated form as a supplement during pregnancy, unless the doctor prescribes it. Instead, you can basically take beta carotene. Once a day, eat raw freshly grated apples, carrots, lemon juice, a teaspoon of wheat-germ oil and honey in a natural state. For the first four months, here is a remedy for strengthening the nerves: four teaspoons of fresh onion juice mixed with honey in a natural state, to be taken over the course of the day; melissa tea with honey also works. Starting about eight weeks before the birth, have a cup of honey-sweetened tea made from equal parts of blackberry leaves and lady's mantle. Caraway tea can

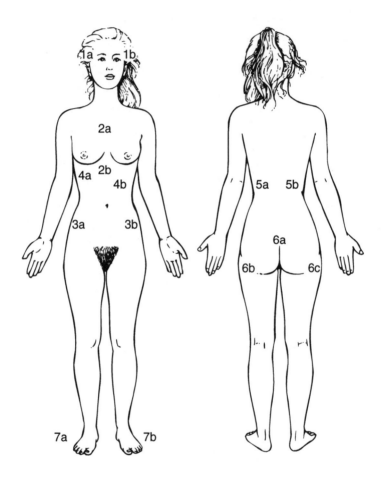

Treatment positions:

1a,b) Temples; 2a) heart, 2b) solar plexus; 3a,b) pelvic V; 4a) liver, 4b) spleen/pancreas; 5a,b) kidneys; 6a) sacrum, 6b) connection to thigh on the right outer leg 6c) like 6b) only on the left side; 7a,b) soles of the feet, toe tips to foot middle.

also be recommended as both teas strengthen and relax the organs involved in birth.

During breast-feeding: Milk production is promoted by dill-seed or caraway tea. Please note: All measures done on a regular basis during the birth and breast-feeding period should be discussed with the attending physician/naturopath to be on the safe side!

Visit to the doctor/healing practitioner: Next to the normal obligatory gynecological care, an experienced naturopath can be of considerable help for the mother and child.

Visit to a psychotherapist: Only useful when intense emotional crises occur or major problems already existed beforehand.

Prostate Problems

General: There are many reasons for prostate disorders, such as bacterial infections, urinary-tract infections, tooth-root purulence, psychological strain continuing over a longer period of time, gout, chill, an excessive amount of sexual intercourse—but also celibacy. Energetically, the first and second chakras are responsible for the prostate. Become informed about their functions and clarify which of them you have perhaps not yet integrated harmoniously into your life.

Reiki treatment with 1st degree: Give the following positions over a longer time every day for at least ten minutes each—1a) sacrum, 1b) from beneath the coccyx to perineum; 2a,b) above the gluteal muscle; 3a,b) pelvic V; lay the hands to form a V from the pelvic bones to the pubic bone; 4a) solar plexus, 4b) navel.

Reiki treatment with 2nd degree: Mental healing with affirmations. Reiki for the *higher self.*

Natural-healing supplement: Drink at least three glasses of kombucha and take wheat-grass juice* (2-3 tbsp. of juice 3 times a day). Eat asparagus, but only if you don't have a disposition toward rheumatism or arthritis. As prevention and a supplement when afflicted, eat pumpkin seeds and pumpkin. Use pumpkin-seed oil. Eliminate alcohol and meat. Use only raw-milk products.

Visit to a doctor/healing practitioner: It is absolutely essential that prostate complaints be exactly diagnosed immediately and treated by a doctor. Natural-healing methods are very effective here. A visit to an osteopath is also useful in this case.

Visit to a psychotherapist: Only in very stubborn cases is this appropriate. Prostate complaints can be an expression of the "male menopause."

---

*Or any other drink containing chlorophyll, such as "Kyo-Green" (see suppliers on page 153).

Prostate Problems

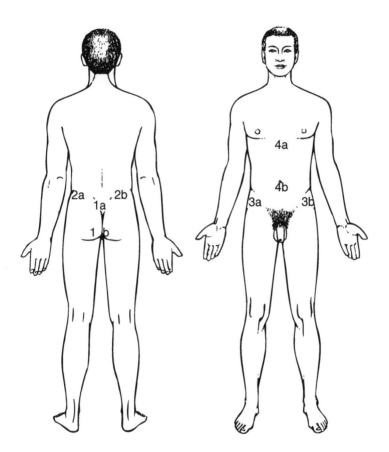

Treatment positions:

1a) Sacrum, 1b) from beneath the coccyx to the perineum; 2a,b) above the gluteal muscle; 3a,b) pelvic V; 4a) solar plexus, 4b) navel.

Rheumatism

General: Rheumatism is a general term for disorders of the locomotor system. It can occur in an acute or a chronic form. It is usually caused by a combination of unfavorable circumstances in life and a hereditary disposition.

Reiki treatment with 1st degree: Give the following positions over a longer period of time every day for at least five minutes each—1a) forehead with third eye, 1b) back of head with medulla oblongata; 2a) solar plexus, 2b) liver; 3a,b) pelvic V, lay the hands in the form of a V from the pelvic bones to the pubic bone; 4a,b) kidneys; 5a,b) hollow of the knee; 6a,b) soles of the feet from the tips of the toes to the middle of the foot. As an additional measure, use on the places where there is intense pain. As often as possible in between times, give positions 1a,b) and 2a,b).

Reiki treatment with 2nd degree: Mental treatment with suggestions. In difficult cases, also use Reiki for the *inner child* and *higher self* to support a long-term change.

Natural-healing supplement: Drink several glasses of kombucha several times a day and wheat-grass juice* (2-3 tbsp.) three times a day. Do basic intestinal cleansing under qualified direction. One hour before meals three times a day, drink about 1 liter of fresh celery juice.

Caution: Those with kidney disorders and pregnant women are only allowed to drink celery juice on a regular basis with the express permission of the attending physician. Rub spirit of Carmelite on painful areas. Drink one or two squeezed lemons with honey and water in portions every day.

Visit to a doctor/healing practitioner: It is essential to get an exact diagnosis from an experienced naturopath and, when necessary, undergo the appropriate treatment.

Visit to a psychotherapist: Rarely useful.

---

*Or any other drink containing chlorophyll, such as "Kyo-Green" (see suppliers on page 153).

Rheumatism

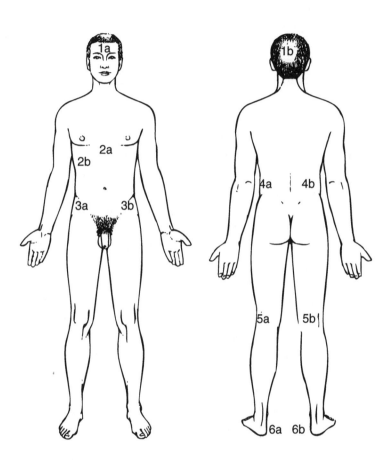

Treatment positions:

1a) Forehead with third eye, 1b) back of the head with medulla oblongata; 2a) solar plexus, 2b) liver; 3a,b) pelvic V; 4a,b) kidneys; 5a,b) hollow of the knees; 6a,b) soles of the feet, tips of the toes to the middle of the foot.

Sciatica

General: Beginning with so-called middle-age, a great many people become afflicted with sciatica. In nine out of ten cases, the cause is a slipped disk or a degenerative illness of parts of the spine. The first and second chakras are the ones responsible in terms of energy.

Reiki treatment with 1st degree: Give the following positions at least fifteen minutes each several times a day until the disorder has subsided—1a) to the right of the sacrum, on upper part of gluteal muscle, 1b) foot sole of the right foot on the heel; 2a) like 1a) but on the left; 2b) like 1b) but on the left; 3a) sacrum. For a long-term reduction of the tendency toward sciatica, treat as above with the given positions even during periods which are free of attacks, additionally treating the lower back area to the left and right of the spine as in 3a) together with 3b) left elbow tip and then 3a) with 3c) right elbow tip.

Reiki treatment with 2nd degree: Give a mental treatment with suggestions and Reiki for the *inner child.*

Natural-healing supplement: Give up alcohol, tobacco and coffee. Up to five times a day, drink a half glass of white-cabbage juice. Apply hot wraps with healing earth, and change about every two hours. Use multi-layered wrap with white-cabbage leaves (for application, look under "Sore Throat"). Think about the question: Why don't you want to be able to walk your path at the moment? What frightens you about it? What makes you angry at the moment, without you expressing it? Learn to do Feldenkrais exercises.

Visit to a doctor/healing practitioner: This is very important since other types of severe illness could be concealed behind these symptoms.

Visit to a psychotherapist: In general, not appropriate.

Sciatica

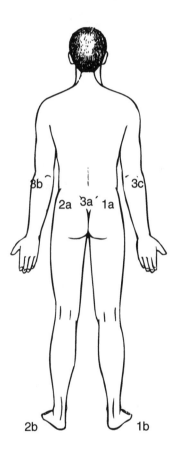

Treatment positions:

1a) To the right of the sacrum, on the upper part of the gluteal muscle, 1b) foot sole of the right foot on the heel; 2a) like 1a) but on the left; 2b) like 1b) but on the left; 3a) sacrum, 3b) tip of left elbow; 3c) tip of right elbow.

Sexual Disturbances

General: Within this context, sexual disturbances are understood to be: a) decreasing or no longer existent inclination toward sexual activity, b) impotence and c) inability to have an orgasm.

Impotence and inability to have an orgasm should be treated by an experienced naturopath and a psychotherapist. If the listlessness should continue for a longer period time, and if it doesn't noticeably improve when the measures outlined below are undertaken, the same applies. Sexuality and the desire for sexual pleasure have a central function in a healthy, natural life. Disturbances in this area must be taken seriously and competently treated. Some medications have side effects that decrease this desire. By the way: a genuine spiritual development without a happy and intensive sexual life is not possible!

Reiki treatment with 1st degree: Give the following positions over a longer period of time every day for at least seven minutes each—1a,b) from the forehead to the teeth parallel to the nose; 2a) solar plexus, at first together with 2b) the hand from the right pelvic bone to the pubic bone and then 2c) like 2b) but on the left; 3a,b) take the crossed hands (because it is more comfortable), palm to palm; 4a,b) kidneys; 5a) sacrum, 5b) from beneath the coccyx to the perineum. In difficult cases, additionally use 6a,b) shoulder blades and 7a,b) tips of elbows.

Reiki treatment with 2nd degree: Mental treatment with suggestions. In difficult cases, also give Reiki for the *inner child* and the *higher self.*

Natural-healing supplement: If no organic damage, personal or relationship problems exist, then lowered sexual drive often comes from overexertion or overwork. Decrease stress and work, so that desire has the room to unfold in your life. Then the following can help: take twenty drops of the homeopathic remedy Damiana1x twice daily, but no longer than fourteen days without the supervision of a naturopath. Drink the

Sexual Disturbances

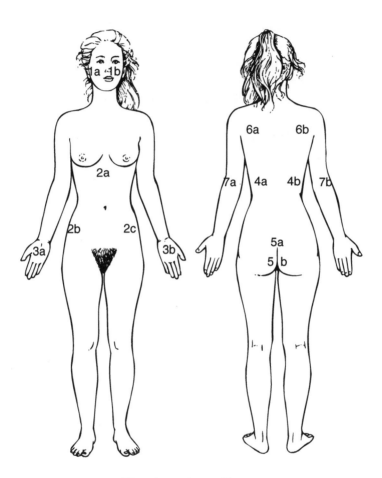

Treatment positions:

1a,b) Forehead to teeth, parallel to the nose; 2a) solar plexus, 2b) the hand from the right pelvic bone to the pubic bone, 2c) like 2b) but on the left; 3a,b) palm; 4a,b) kidneys; 5a) sacrum, 5b) from beneath the coccyx to the perineum; 6a,b) shoulder blades; 7a,b) tips of elbows.

131

following "cocktail" every day: A big glass of fresh white-cabbage juice mixed with a tablespoon of wheat-germ oil, a teaspoon of honey, a tablespoon of apple-cider vinegar, a teaspoon of yeast flakes and fresh dill or ground caraway. Eliminate all stimulants and discuss with your partner how sexual togetherness can be provide more variety and be more exciting for both of you. Experiment and try out new things! Anything that both of you enjoy is permitted.

Visit to a doctor/healing practitioner: Also look under **General**.

Visit to a psychotherapist: Also look under **General**.

Sleep Disturbances

General: Every type of unconquered stress situation, either conscious or unconscious, stimulant abuse, as well as psychological or organic types of illness, can lead to difficulties in falling asleep or sleeping for the entire night. Also look under "Nervousness."

Reiki treatment with 1st degree: Give the following positions over a longer period of time every day for at least seven minutes each in order to lessen the tendency toward sleep disturbances—1a,b) temples; 2a) heart, 2b) solar plexus; 3a,b) pelvic V, lay the hands to form a V from the pelvic bones to the pubic bone; 4a,b) foot soles from the tips of the toes to the middle of the foot. In stubborn cases, give 2b) and 3a,b) as often as possible in between times.

Reiki treatment with 2nd degree: Give mental treatment with suggestions and Reiki for the *inner child.*

Natural-healing supplement: Shortly before going to sleep, drink one glass of apple-peel tea with natural honey. Or instead drink dill-seed tea (25%), green oat tea (50%) and anise (25%), also sweetened with honey. Regularly eat a head of lettuce, as fresh as possible before bedtime. Learn to constructively express feelings which have not been lived out. Resolutely approach problems and make decisions. Leave at least three hours time between the last meal and bedtime and eliminate coffee, chocolate and black tea for a while.

Visit to a doctor/healing practitioner: If there are sleep disturbances over a longer period of time, or if they continue to keep returning periodically, you must absolutely seek qualified naturopathic advice.

Visit to a psychotherapist: This is important in cases of long-lasting sleep disturbances without recognizable organic causes. Whether depression exists also needs to be clarified.

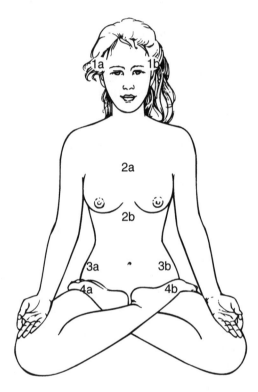

Treatment positions:

1a,b) Temples; 2a) heart, 2b) solar plexus; 3a,b) pelvic V; 4a,b) soles of the feet, toe tips to middle of the foot.

Sore Throat

General: This is mainly caused by a viral infection but can be a reaction to dry air, overexertion of the vocal apparatus or spasms in the throat region. The fifth chakra is energetically responsible. Also look under "Hoarseness."

Reiki treatment with 1st degree: Give the following positions at least two to three times a day for ten minutes each, until the disorder subsides—1a,b) front side of throat, without contact by the hands; 2a) forehead with third eye, 2b) thymus gland beneath the throat; 3a,b) collar-bones; 4a,b) soles of the feet from the toes to the middle of the foot. Alternative: treat 1) and 3) more frequently.

Reiki treatment with 2nd degree: Mental treatment with suggestions. In severe cases, also give Reiki for the *inner child.*

Natural-healing supplement: Gargle with a mixture of wheat bran, honey and water. Briefly boil the wheat bran with plenty of water and then let it cool to below 104 degrees Fahrenheit. Add honey and let steep for about an hour at about 95 degrees Fahrenheit. After straining, you can gargle with it as it is or first dilute it. Drink fennel tea and gargle with it as well. Especially effective is crushed garlic with hot water poured over it. Do throat wraps with moist healing earth or white-cabbage leaves. Don't use the outer leaves. Remove the hard leaf parts and then flatten the rest with a rolling pin until the leaves are soft and juice begins to come out. Gargle with salt water.

Visit to a doctor/healing practitioner: This is only necessary in severe cases or when the sore throat keeps occurring on a regular basis.

Visit to a psychotherapist: Only useful when no organic causes can be found and the usual healing methods haven't worked.

Sore Throat

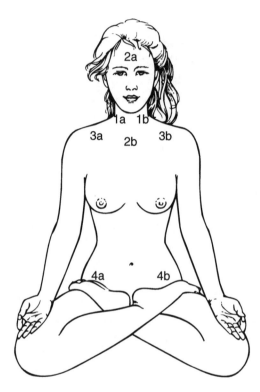

Treatment positions:

1a,b) Front of the throat; 2a) forehead with third eye, 2b) thymus gland; 3a,b) collar-bones; 4a,b) soles of the feet, toes to the middle of the foot.

Sprains

General: Through awkward movements, intense strain of the ligaments, hydrarthrosis of the joints, changes in the shape of the joints and more sprains can occur. Among other things, this can cause considerable pain and a limitation of movement. You should take sprains very seriously!

Reiki treatment with 1st degree: Treat the sprain as quickly as possible and then for at least thirty minutes. The pain will initially increase during the effect of the Reiki and then recede again. In any case, wait for this reaction and then continue the treatment for at least another fifteen minutes. Then give Reiki at least three times a day for about twenty minutes at a time until the sprain is healed.

Reiki treatment with 2nd degree: In cases where there is a disposition toward injury, give mental treatment with suggestions and Reiki for the *inner child.*

Natural-healing supplement: Apply an "alcohol bandage." Soak a bandage, a handkerchief or something similar in a high-proof alcohol (at least 45% to 60%, but dilute if it is stronger) and lay it on the affected area and fix it in place with a bandage. Change every three to four hours. Also to be recommended are arnica ointment, Rescue Remedy from Bach flower essences and Symphytum externum. Furthermore, apply compresses with fresh white-cabbage leaves. Prepare in the manner described under "Teeth." Keep injury still and don't put any weight on it.

Visit to a doctor/healing practitioner: Should always occur when sprains are more than trivial injuries to be sure that nothing is broken or severely injured in any other manner, and when it is necessary to have a splint.

Visit to a psychotherapist: Only useful when sprains keep reoccurring at short intervals (disposition to injury!).

Stomach Irritation

General: Stomach irritations occur as a result of acute causes like the misuse of stimulants. However, they can also be triggered by medication or food poisoning or intolerance of foods. If stomach irritations occur frequently, they can also indicate excessive psychological strain, fears, insecurity, worry, over-exertion, or some type of organic illness. In energetic terms, the third chakra is responsible.

Reiki treatment with 1st degree: Treat the area of the stomach several times a day for at least fifteen minutes and additionally the entire abdominal area. In severe cases, also do the middle of the foot sole of both feet and the back of the head.

Reiki treatment with 2nd degree: Mental treatment with suggestions, in chronic cases also give Reiki for the *inner child.*

Natural-healing supplement: Get silicea balsam at the health-food store or pharmacy. It is the *best* remedy for stomach irritation and has an equally beneficial effect medicinally and symptomatically. In acute and chronic cases, freshly pressed white-cabbage juice with a little finely minced dill or ground caraway is also very good. "Ultra" healing earth is very helpful. If you don't have any of these at home, black tea without anything added will do the trick. If a person doesn't want to fast during the healing (which can be highly recommended), freshly prepared mashed potatoes in different variations can sooth the stomach and also contribute to healing.

Visit to a doctor/healing practitioner: In severely acute and chronic cases, it is absolutely necessary to consult an experienced naturopath so that an exact diagnosis can be made and—when necessary—an appropriate therapy initiated.

Visit to a psychotherapist: Useful in stubborn cases.

Tennis Arm

General: Tennis arm occurs in the following manner: When the elbow joints are excessively strained, damage occurs there. This leads to further tears to the tendons. Pain caused by pressure can also appear, which can additionally radiate as muscle tightness. But why does this happen? The reason may be too much exertion in sports or a basically false way of moving, combined with a long-term energetic weakness in the area of the elbow. There is also an energetic connection to the pancreas and important secondary chakras are located on the elbow.

Reiki treatment with 1st degree: Grasp the affected elbow and the hand from the same arm, so that the hands are palm to palm. Instead of the palm, then grasp the shoulder, leaving the rest of the position the way it was. For long-lasting changes, treat the entire head-shoulder-neck area. In the following weeks, continue to give Reiki as often as possible to the place where a particularly strong need for energy was determined after the first treatment. Don't do the other positions. Aside from that, give at least ten minutes each a day of the following positions— 1a) solar plexus and 1b) spleen/pancreas.

Reiki treatment with 2nd degree: Mental treatment with suggestions (effective on a medium to long-term basis).

Natural-healing supplement: Learn new, harmonious movement patterns such as the Feldenkrais method or the Alexander technique. Both exercise systems cannot be learned from books. But today there are courses on them practically everywhere. An acute case can be reasonably relieved with cold healing-earth compresses. Use cold water to mix the earth into a paste which can be spread, then spread it on a cloth, wrap around the elbow and use another cloth to bind it in place. Also helpful is a multi-layered wrap of white-cabbage leaves, which should be left on for several hours. Look under "Teeth" for how this is made.

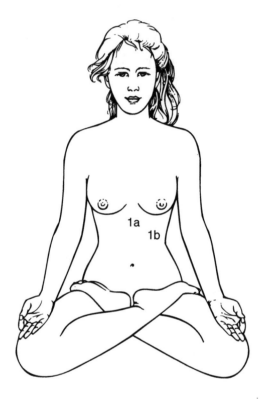

Treatment positions:

1a) Solar plexus, 1b) spleen/pancreas.

Visit to a doctor/healing practitioner: Qualified naturopathic advice must be sought in stubborn and difficult cases.

Visit to a psychotherapist: Not appropriate.

Teeth/Cavities/Pain

General: Tooth problems of all kinds, including periodontal, are practically always an expression of a larger disharmony within the total organism. Every tooth has a connection to meridians and organs. If these are imbalanced for a longer period of time, the tooth will be more easily damaged.* The teeth with the fixation apparatus can basically be assigned to the first and, in part, to the third chakra. Disharmonies in these energy centers for longer period of time always fundamentally lead to tooth trouble at some point.

Reiki treatment with 1st degree: Directly treat the teeth several times a day for at least ten minutes. Also give the following positions over a longer period of time for ten minutes each in order to achieve a fundamental change—1a) sacrum, 1b) from beneath the coccyx to the perineum; 2a,b) from the prominent cervical vertebrae at the shoulder to the front; 3a,b) soles of the feet from the toe tips to the middle of the foot.

Reiki treatment with 2nd degree: Mental treatment with suggestions. In cases with wide reaching problems, also give Reiki for the *inner child*.

Natural-healing supplement: Switch to high-quality nutrition to get a better supply of vital substances. However, this is only useful if at the same time the metabolism and the disturbed organs, particularly the digestive area, are brought back in harmony by a naturopath. In cases of neuralgic toothache, apply fresh white-cabbage leaves (not the outer ones!). Wash beforehand with lukewarm water, and soften them so that the juice comes out, for example, with a rolling pin. From pain due to cavities, you can bridge the time until you see the dentist by putting cloves, fresh garlic or ginger pieces on the affected spot. In cases of gum disorders, spread natural honey

*In my "The Complete Reiki Handbook", under the catchphrase 'Teeth' in the list of Special Poisitions, the order of the meridians are listed.

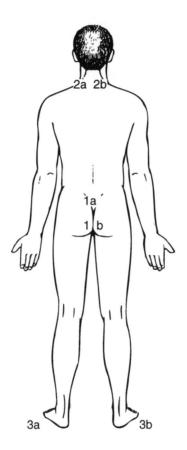

Treatment positions:

1a) Sacrum, 1b) from beneath the coccyx to the perineum; 2a,b) from the prominent cervical vertebrae at the shoulder to the front; 3a,b) foot soles, toe tips to the middle of the foot.

on the area at regular intervals and drink a glass of warm water with a good teaspoon of honey and a tablespoon of silicea balsam (available in health-food stores and pharmacies) every morning before breakfast. The kombucha and the wheat-grass juice* (2-3 tbsp. of juice 3 times a day) can also be strongly recommended. Everything should be taken over a longer period of time—months!

Visit to a doctor/healing practitioner: Try to find a dentist who works with natural-healing methods. Optimal would be a combined effort, with a general naturopath tending to the elimination of the underlying organic/energetic disharmonies.

Visit to a psychotherapist: Only useful in stubborn cases to harmonize the relationship between aggression and self-confidence, the ability to assert oneself and the sense of self-worth.

---

*Or any other drink containing chlorophyll, such as "Kyo-Green" (see suppliers on page 153).

Warts

General: Warts are defined as benign infectious tissue tumors in the top layer of the skin. They are probably the body's reaction to a viral infection. Localized circulation disorders promote the growth of warts. People who tend to get them because of disorders of the vegetative system or due to other reasons, get them with a much higher frequency. Warts on the feet are frequently confused with clavi (corns)! Both are basically treated in a very different manner.

Reiki treatment with 1st degree: Treat the warts directly for at least ten minutes every day. Also, for a longer period of time every day, treat the entire stomach and pelvic region for at least thirty minutes to achieve a basic change.

Reiki treatment with 2nd degree: Do mental healing with affirmations and Reiki for the *inner child.*

Natural-healing supplement: A cure by means of incantation has very good prospects for success. If you don't know anyone who does this, try it yourself with the following folk-remedy method: During the waning moon, take a small bowl, which is not made of plastic or metal, and some water, and go out into nature. Look at the moon and ask the Creative Power and the Moon Goddess for their help and their blessings for the healing. Explain in your prayer why you want to be healed. During the whole time, hold your hand over the bowl filled with water. Sense within yourself for awhile after the prayer and perceive how the water sends out increasingly stronger healing vibrations. Then dip the middle finger of one hand into the water and sprinkle every wart with it. While doing this, say: "The Creative Power gives, the Creative Power takes. Return to the source of your being and become pure there!". Afterward, pour the water into nature and bury the bowl. Under no circumstances should you constantly check to see if the ritual has already started to work! The more you occupy yourself with other things, the better the effect will be. Further possibilities: Rub the wart(s) with castor oil several times a day. Every third day, put a bandage over the wart with fresh ginger or garlic, which has natural honey spread on the contact surface so that it sticks to the wart. Change twice a day. Calendula leaves or ointment applied overnight are helpful as well. Also look under "Immune-System Deficiencies" and "Detoxification."

Visit to a doctor/healing practitioner: Acupuncture or acupressure, Bach flower essences and classic homeopathy are frequently helpful. Cutting, burning away or cauterizing warts is not to be recommended. There are enough other more humanitarian, very effective healing methods.

Visit to a psychotherapist: Only in totally stubborn cases that continually return after appearing to be healed is a visit useful.

Wounds

General and natural-healing supplement: Give Reiki immediately for about fifteen minutes for all types of small wounds. Under no circumstances should you touch the wound while doing so. The pain will initially get stronger, and then it will subside. After it does so, continue to treat it for at least five minutes—in cases of larger, older or unclean wounds, for a much longer period of time. Bandage or wrap in a normal manner with calendula ointment, for example. A good natural honey is also an excellent help, even for dirty wounds. It inhibits inflammation, promotes healing and is full of life energy! When it is used, the wound will usually heal very quickly. Instead of honey, you can also use healing earth or kombucha. For larger injuries and the resulting wound treatment, the general treatment as well as a visit to a doctor or healing practitioner is important. Pay attention to regulation of the bowel movement, a low-sodium diet, raw foods, and in cases of strong wound secretion, a diet of dry food. (Also see "Bleeding" and "Burns".)

Reiki treatment with 1st degree: The affected body areas should basically be supplied with Reiki as often as possible. Whole-body treatments are useful every second or third day, if larger injuries are involved.

Reiki treatment with 2nd degree: Through mental treatment with selected suggestions, the tendency toward self-destructiveness can be healed and the life flow directed into more peaceful paths. This is only necessary in the case of an obvious tendency toward injury.

Visit to a doctor/healing practitioner: Look under **General**.

Index I

Annotated Bibliography

Reiki

"**The Complete Reiki Handbook**" by Walter Lübeck, Lotus Light Publications. A detailed introduction oriented toward the practice of Reiki healing. There is an extensive ABC of special positions, as well as advice concerning Reiki and medication, Reiki meditation, work with precious stones and aromatherapy.

"**Reiki—The Path of the Heart**" by Walter Lübeck, Lotus Light Publications. This book is an introduction to Reiki-Do, the advancement of spiritual development and happiness in life with Reiki. It offers a history of the Reiki tradition, instructions for practical use of the guiding principles and exact descriptions of the possibilities of the different degrees of Reiki. This book will be soon published by Lotus Light, Shangri-La Series.

"**Empowerment Through Reiki**" by Paula Horan, Lotus Light Publications. This is an important book about Reiki because it describes many of the ideas of holistic medicine in relation to Reiki.

The Subtle Energy System

"**The Chakra Handbook**" by Baginski/Sharamon, Lotus Light Publications. This is an excellent work about the functions of the seven main chakras with many exercises, classification tables and thought-provoking ideas.

"**The Body of Light**" by Mann/Short, Charles E. Tuttle, Boston. This is a very interesting introduction to various ways in which the great spiritual traditions look at the inner energy system.

Nutrition

"**The Beverly Hills Diet**" by Judy Mazel, self-published. This book is excellent in both content and method. If you are considering a diet which you want to be healthy, taste good and have a plenty of variety and practicality for everyday use, try this one. Also suitable for vegetarians, although you'll have to eliminate some things and tailor it to your needs.

"**The Ayurvedic Cookbook**" by Amadea Morningstar and Urmila Desai, Lotus Light Publications and "**Ayurvedic Cooking for Westerners**" by Amadea Morningstar, Lotus Light Publications. These are both excellent books about the old Indian tradition of healing, nutrition and rejuvenation—also suitable for vegetarians.

"**Ayurveda—The Science of Self-Healing**" by Vasant Lad, Lotus Light Publications. This book is an excellent introduction to the Indian philosophical principles of healing and nutrition, with a detaild discussion of diagnostic techniques and treatments.

"**The Yoga of Herbs**" by Vasant Lad and David Frawley. This book is excellent in both content and method. Lists Western herbs and spices used for healing.

Biochemistry and Homeopathy

"**Biochemie—Eine Volksheilweise**" ("Biochemistry—A Folk Method of Treatment") by Dr. H.G. Jaedikke, Alwin Fröhlich Verlag. This book is a good introduction into the biochemistry developed by Dr. Schussler. This is a sort of miniature edition of the "Hahnemann homeopathy". "Biochemistry" is a wonderful holistic medicine chest for the lay person.

Metamorphic Method

"**The Metamorphic Technique, Principles and Practice**" by Gaston St. Pierre and Debbie Boater, Element Books Ltd., and "**Metamorphosis—A Textbook on Prenatal Therapy**" by

Robert St. John, self-published, are two books about a fantastic self-help method which you absolutely must read. Alone and in combination with Reiki, they will open up for new worlds you.

Organic-Ecological Nutrition

"The Secrets of the Soil" by Tompkins/Bird, Harper. Some years ago, Tompkins and Bird wrote the best-seller "The Secret Life of Plants." Their new book is perhaps even more important. Through correct behavior in terms of our nutrition, it shows us possibilities to help re-balance our planet's ecological system, as well as our own body and spirit.

Everyday Life as a Spiritual Exercise

"The Secret Way of Wonder" by Guy Finley, Llewellyn, Public., St. Paul. This book describes discovering the world with the eyes of a child and thereby making healing and growth possible.

Anatomy and Reflexology

"Life Energy" by Dr. John Diamond, self-published. This book discusses kinesiology in reference to acupuncture meridians, reflex zones for testing and treatment and shows an interesting correlation to biochemistry.

Index II

Overview of Curative Foods in Relation to Organs and Functions

To help you deal creatively with healing foods, I have compiled a list related to organs and functions in the following text.

In the practice, by all means please pay attention to these rules: Plants which have been overbred, grown under unnatural conditions, been stored for a long period of time, are not used fresh, as well fruits and vegetables which have been exposed to large shifts in temperature usually have very little healing power. However, if they come from organic-ecological cultivation, are used around the actual time of harvesting and are not been exposed to large temperature shifts, they have immense healing power! The shamanistic ritual described at the beginning of Chapter Four can even intensify their effects. For severe or long-lasting disorders, please always inform the attending naturopathic doctor about the applications since individual situations can be encountered which not even the most complete book can address. Here is the list:

Liver/Gallbladder: Wheat germ;, honey; whole-grain rice; dandelion; stinging nettle; radish; strawberry.

Kidneys: Strawberry; thyme (anti-inflammatory); carrots; oats; fennel; cucumber; pumpkin and squash.

Lungs: Oats; honey; stinging nettle; onions; horseradish.

Pancreas: Dandelion; tomatoes; for relieving the insulin-building function: topinambour and bean-pod tea.

Stomach: Dandelion; tomatoes; very freshly prepared white cabbage (and juice); anise; wheat; silicea balsam.

General metabolism: Pumpkin and squash; onions; garlic;

carrots; white cabbage; sauerkraut (and juice); kombucha, wheat-grass juice*; honey.

Intestines/digestion: Kefir; yogurt; kombucha; sauerkraut juice; silicea balsam; honey.

Psyche: St. John's wort; melissa; garlic; valerian; kombucha; oats.

Detoxification from radioactivity and healing of the damage it causes: Miso; lettuce; stinging nettle; kombucha.

---

*Or any other drink containing chlorophyll, such as "Kyo-Green" (see suppliers on page 153).

Addresses and Sources of Supply

Wholesale
(Contact with your business name, resale number
or practicioner license)

LOTUS LIGHT
PO BOX 1008 AR
Silver Lake, WI 53170
414/889-8501
Fax 414/889-8591

Retail
Lotus Filfillment Service
33719 116th Street Box AR
Twin Lakes WI 53181

About the Author

Walter Lubeck is a renowned Reiki master, founder and director of the Reiki-Do Institute. He is a bestselling prolific author of classic works on Reiki, as well as books on other healing methods, such as work with Chakra balancing, pendulums, and auras. In the last years he has developed a method he refers to as Rainbow Reiki which includes an unlimited spectrum of applications like channeling, astral travel, making Reiki essences, therapy with precious stones, as well as personality development and wholistic enviromental protection. He has spent many years studying diverse martial arts, meditation, natural healing and energy work of all kinds. Walter Lubeck orients himself in his entire work toward three basic principles: support of personal individual responsibility, development of the ability to love, and conciousness expansion. His goal is to contribute to the betterment of the quality of daily life through spiritual knowledge and thereby to bring man, nature and God in harmony. He lives with his wife, the philospher and shaman Greta Bahya, and child in Weserbergland, Germany in a landscape filled with ancient power spots.

If you would like to contact **Walter Lübeck** and *The Reiki Do Institute*, please write to:

Windpferd Verlag
"Reiki for First Aid"
Friesenrieder Straße 45
87648 Aitrang

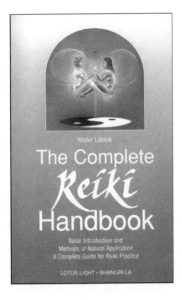

Walter Lübeck

The Complete Reiki Handbook

Basic Introduction and Methods of Natural Application. A Complete Guide for Reiki Practice

This handbook is a complete guide for Reiki practice and a wonderful tool for the necessary adjustment to the changes inherent in a new age. The author's style of natural simplicity, so beloved by the readers of his many bestselling books, wonderfully complements this basic method for accessing universal life energy. He shares with us, as only such a Reiki master can, the personal experience accumulated in his years of practice. The lovely illustrations of the different positons make the information as easily visually accessible, as does the author's direct and undogmatic style. This work also offers a synthesis of Reiki and many other popular forms of healing.

192 pages, $ 14.95
ISBN 0-941524-87-6

Shalila Sharamon and Bodo J. Baginski

The Chakra-Handbook

From basic understanding to practical application

Knowledge of the energy centers provides us with deep, comprehensive insight into the effects the subtle powers have on the human organism. This book vividly describes the functioning of the energy centers. For practical work with the chakras this book offers a wealth of possibilities: the application of sounds, colors, gemstones and fragrances with their own specific effects, augmented by meditation, breathing techniques, foot reflexology massage of the chakra points and the instilling of universal life energy. The description of nature experiences, yoga practices and the relationship of each indiviual chakra to the Zodiac additionally provides inspiring and valuable insight.

192 pages, $ 14,95
ISBN 0-941524-85-X

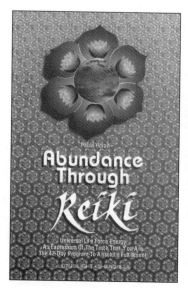

Paula Horan

Abundance Through Reiki

Universal Life Force Energy As Expression Of The Truth That You Are. The 42-Day Program To Absolute Fulfillment

A book that goes right to the core of your abundance issues. A timeless jewel, full of insights for the Golden Age of Now.

Abundance Through Reiki is a powerful, poetic evocation of true Self and Universal Life Force Energy. At the heart of the book are the 42 steps from Core Self to Core Abundance, creating richness within and without. They are presented in detail in the form of two very different finely tuned 21-day abundance plans, taking you on an exploration of some of your belief patterns, which keep you from experiencing all the things you need or desire in your life.

160 pages, $14,95
ISBN 0-914955-25-X

Paula Horan

Empowerment Through Reiki

The Path to Personal and Global Transformation

In a gentle and loving manner, Paula Horan, world renowned Reiki master and bestselling author, offers a clear explanation of Reiki energy and its healing effects. This text is a must for the experienced practitioner. The reader is lead through the history of this remarkable healing work to the practical application of it through simple exercises. We are not only supplied with a deep understanding of the Reiki principles, but with an approach to this energy in combination with other basic healing like Chakra balancing, massage and work with tones, colors and crystals. This handbook truly offers us personal transformation, so necessary for the global transformation of the millenial change.

160 pages, $ 14.95
ISBN 0-941524-84-1

Magie Tisserand · Monika Jünemann

The Magic and Power of Lavender

The Secret of the „Blue Flower"

The scent of lavender, in a way, has permeated whole regions of Europe, contributing to their special character, and it has dominated perfumery for most of its history. To this very day lavender has remained one of the most familiar, popular and utilised of all fragrances.

This book introduces you to the delightful and enticing secrets of this plant and its essence, demonstrating its healing power, while also presenting to you the places and people involved in its cultivation. The authors have asked doctors, holistic health practitioners, chemists, and perfumers about their experiences and take this opportunity to share their own experiences with you.

136 pages, $ 9,95
ISBN 0-941524-88-4

Rodolphe Balz

The Healing Power of Essential Oils

Fragrance Secrets for Everyday Use. This handbook is a compact reference work on the effects and applications of 248 essential oils for health, fitness, and well-being

Fifteen years of organic cultivation of spice plants and healing herbs in the French Provence have provided Rodolphe Balz with extensive knowledge about essential oils, how they work, and how to use them.

The heart of *The Healing Power of Essential Oils* is an essenial-oil index describing their properties, followed by a comprehensive therapeutic index for putting them to practical use. Further topics of this indispensible aromatherapy handbook are distillation processes, concentrations, chemotypes, quality and quality control, toxicity, self-medication, and the aromatogram.

208 pages, $ 14.95
ISBN 0-941524-89-2

Marianne Uhl

Chakra Energy Massage

Spiritual evolution into the Subconscious through activation of the energy points of the feet

This book guides you into the fascinating world of the energy body. Drawing on the knowledge gained by Foot Reflexology Massage it introduces you to Chakra Energy Massage, by which the individual energy centers of the human body can be activated. By means of the fine energy channels connecting them to the body's organs and energy centers, our feet reflect our physical and psychic condition. The author enables you to quickly acquire all of the knowledge needed for Foot Reflexology Massage and Chakra Energy Massage. Beyond this she provides information on the vibrations of primal tones and various colors to effectively enhance your work with the chakras.

128 pages, $ 9,95
ISBN 0-941524-83-3

Monika Jünemann

Enchanting Scents

The Secrets of Aroma Therapy Fragrant essences that stimulate, activate and inspire body, mind and spirit

Today we are as captivated by the magic of lovely scents and as irresistably moved by them as ever. The effects that essential oils have can vary greatly. This book particularly treats their subtle influences, but also presents and describes the plants from which they are obtained. Enchanting Scents beckons you to enter the realm of sensual experience, to journey into the world of fragrance through essences. It is an invitation to employ personal scents, to activate body and spirit. Here is a key that will open your senses to the limitless possibilities of benefitting from fragrances as stimulators, sources of energy and means of healing.

128 pages, $ 9,95
ISBN 0-941524-36-1

BIOMAGNETIC
and Herbal Therapy
Dr. Michael Tierra

$10.95   96 pp
5 3/8 x 8 1/2 quality trade paper
ISBN 0-914955-33-0

Magnetic energy is the structural force of the universe. In this book the respected herbalist and healer, Dr. Michael Tierra enlightens us on the healing influence of commercially available magnets for many conditions and describes the sometimes miraculous relief from such problems as joint pain, skin diseases, acidity, blood pressure, tumors, kidney, liver and thyroid problems, and more. Magnetizing herbs, teas, water and their usage in conjunction with direct placement of magnets for synergistic effectiveness is presented in a systematic, succinct and practical manner for the benefit of the professional and lay person alike. Replete with diagrams, and appendices, this is a "how to do" practical handbook for augmenting health and obtaining relief from pain.

The paradigm of health in the future is based on energy flow. This paradigm reaches back to the ancient healing arts of the traditional Chinese, the Ayurvedic and the Native American cultures. It is connected to the work of Hippocrates, the "father" of Western medicine, in ancient Greek culture, and found its way through the herbal and homeopathic science that has flourished in Europe over the last few hundred years.

Dr. Tierra is the author of the all-time best selling herbal *The Way of Herbs* as well as the synthesizing work *Planetary Herbology*. He is a practicing herbalist and educator in the field with a background of studies spanning the Chinese and Ayurvedic, the Native American and the European herbal traditions.

To order your copy, ask your local bookseller or send
$10.95 + 3.00 (s/h) to:
Lotus Press
P O Box 325 FA
Twin Lakes, Wi 53181 USA

Request our complete book and alternative health products catalogs
of over 7000 items. Wholesale inquiries welcome.

Sources of Supply:

The following companies have an extensive selection of useful products and a long track-record of fulfillment. They have natural body care, aromatherapy, flower essences, crystals and tumbled stones, homeopathy, herbal products, vitamins and supplements, videos, books, audio tapes, candles, incense and bulk herbs, teas, massage tools and products and numerous alternative health items across a wide range of categories.

WHOLESALE:

Wholesale suppliers sell to stores and practitioners, not to individual consumers buying for their own personal use. Individual consumers should contact the RETAIL supplier listed below. Wholesale accounts should contact with business name, resale number or practitioner license in order to obtain a wholesale catalog and set up an account.

Lotus Light Enterprises, Inc.

P O Box 1008 FA
Silver Lake, WI 53170 USA
414 889 8501 (phone)
414 889 8591 (fax)
800 548 3824 (toll free order line)

RETAIL:

Retail suppliers provide products by mail order direct to consumers for their personal use. Stores or practitioners should contact the wholesale supplier listed above.

Internatural

33719 116th Street FA
Twin Lakes, WI 53181 USA
800 643 4221 (toll free order line)
414 889 8581 office phone
WEB SITE: www.internatural.com

Web site includes an extensive annotated catalog of more than 7000 products that can be ordered "on line" for your convenience 24 hours a day, 7 days a week.